THAI VOCABULARY
for English speakers

T&P Books vocabularies are intended to help you learn, memorize, and review foreign words. The vocabulary contains over 3000 commonly used words arranged thematically.

- Vocabulary contains the most commonly used words
- Recommended as an addition to any language course
- Meets the needs of beginners and advanced learners of foreign languages
- Convenient for daily use, revision sessions, and self-testing activities
- Allows you to assess your vocabulary

Special features of the vocabulary

- Words are organized according to their meaning, not alphabetically
- Words are presented in three columns to facilitate the reviewing and self-testing processes
- Words in groups are divided into small blocks to facilitate the learning process
- The vocabulary offers a convenient and simple transcription of each foreign word

The vocabulary has 101 topics including:

Basic Concepts, Numbers, Colors, Months, Seasons, Units of Measurement, Clothing & Accessories, Food & Nutrition, Restaurant, Family Members, Relatives, Character, Feelings, Emotions, Diseases, City, Town, Sightseeing, Shopping, Money, House, Home, Office, Working in the Office, Import & Export, Marketing, Job Search, Sports, Education, Computer, Internet, Tools, Nature, Countries, Nationalities and more ...

TABLE OF CONTENTS

PRONUNCIATION GUIDE

T&P phonetic alphabet	Thai example	English example

Vowels

[a]	ห้า [hâ:] – hâa	shorter than in ask
[e]	เป็นลม [pen lom] – bpen lom	elm, medal
[i]	วินัย [wiʔ naj] – wi–nai	shorter than in feet
[o]	โกน [ko:n] – gohn	pod, John
[u]	ขุนเคือง [kʰùn kʰɯ:aŋ] – khùn kheuang	book
[aa]	ราคา [ra: kʰa:] – raa–khaa	calf, palm
[oo]	ภูมิใจ [pʰu:m tɕaj] – phoom jai	pool, room
[ee]	บัญชี [ban tɕʰi:] – ban–chee	feet, meter
[eu]	เดือน [dɯ:an] – deuan	similar to a longue schwa sound
[er]	เงิน [ŋɤn] – ngern	e in "the"
[ae]	แปล [plɛ:] – bplae	longer than bed, fell
[ay]	เลข [lê:k] – lâyk	longer than in bell
[ai]	ไปป์ [paj] – bpai	time, white
[oi]	โพย [pʰo:j] – phoi	oil, boy, point
[ya]	สัญญา [sǎn ja:] – sǎn–yaa	Kenya, piano
[oie]	อบเชย [ʔòp tɕʰɤ:j] – òp–choie	Combination [ə:i]
[ieo]	หน้าเชียว [nâ: si:aw] – nâa sieow	year, here

Initial consonant sounds

[b]	บาง [ba:ŋ] – baang	baby, book
[d]	สีแดง [sǐ: dɛ:ŋ] – sěe daeng	day, doctor
[f]	มันฝรั่ง [man fà ràŋ] – man fà–ràng	face, food
[h]	เฮลซิงกิ [he:n siŋ kiʔ] – hayn–sing–gì	home, have
[y]	ยี่สิบ [jî: sìp] – yêe sìp	yes, New York
[g]	กรง [kroŋ] – gromg	game, gold
[kh]	เลขา [le: kʰǎ:] – lay–khǎa	work hard
[l]	เล็ก [lék] – lék	lace, people
[m]	เมลอน [me: lɔ:n] – may–lorn	magic, milk
[n]	หนัง [nǎŋ] – nǎng	name, normal
[ng]	เงือก [ŋɯ:ak] – ngêuak	English, ring
[bp]	เป็น [pen] – bpen	pencil, private
[ph]	เผ่า [pʰàw] – phào	top hat

T&P phonetic alphabet	Thai example	English example
[r]	เบอร์รี่ [bɤː rîː] – ber–rêe	rice, radio
[s]	ซ่อน [sôn] – sôrn	city, boss
[dt]	ดนตรี [don triː] – don–dtree	tourist, trip
[j]	ปั้นจั่น [pân tɕàn] – bpân jàn	cheer
[ch]	วิชา [wíʔ tɕʰaː] – wí–chaa	hitchhiker
[th]	แถว [tʰɛːw] – thăe	don't have
[w]	เคียว [kʰiːaw] – khieow	vase, winter

Final consonant sounds

[k]	แม่เหล็ก [mɛː lèk] – mâe lèk	clock, kiss
[m]	เพิ่ม [pʰɤːm] – phêrm	magic, milk
[n]	เนียน [niːan] – nian	name, normal
[ng]	เป็นห่วง [pen hùːaŋ] – bpen hùang	English, ring
[p]	ไม่ขยับ [mâj kʰà ja p] – mâi khà–yàp	pencil, private
[t]	ลูกเป็ด [lûːk pèt] – lôok bpèt	tourist, trip

Comments

Mid tone - [ă] การดูคน [gaan khon]
Low tone - [à] แจกจ่าย [jàek jàai]
Falling tone - [â] แต่ม [dtâem]
High tone - [á] แซ็กโซโฟน [sáek-soh-fohn]
Rising tone - [ǎ] เนินเขา [nern khǎo]

ABBREVIATIONS
used in the vocabulary

English abbreviations

ab.	-	about
adj	-	adjective
adv	-	adverb
anim.	-	animate
as adj	-	attributive noun used as adjective
e.g.	-	for example
etc.	-	et cetera
fam.	-	familiar
fem.	-	feminine
form.	-	formal
inanim.	-	inanimate
masc.	-	masculine
math	-	mathematics
mil.	-	military
n	-	noun
pl	-	plural
pron.	-	pronoun
sb	-	somebody
sing.	-	singular
sth	-	something
v aux	-	auxiliary verb
vi	-	intransitive verb
vi, vt	-	intransitive, transitive verb
vt	-	transitive verb

BASIC CONCEPTS

1. Pronouns

you	คุณ	khun
he	เขา	khăo
she	เธอ	ther
it	มัน	man
we	เรา	rao
you (to a group)	คุณทั้งหลาย	khun tháng lăai
you (polite, sing.)	คุณ	khun
you (polite, pl)	คุณทั้งหลาย	khun tháng lăai
they (masc.)	เขา	khăo
they (fem.)	เธอ	ther

2. Greetings. Salutations

Hello! (fam.)	สวัสดี!	sà-wàt-dee
Hello! (form.)	สวัสดี ครับ/ค่ะ!	sà-wàt-dee khráp/khâ
Good morning!	อรุณสวัสดิ์!	a-run sà-wàt
Good afternoon!	สวัสดีตอนบ่าย	sà-wàt-dee dtorn-bàai
Good evening!	สวัสดีตอนค่ำ	sà-wàt-dee dtorn-khâm
to say hello	ทักทาย	thák thaai
Hi! (hello)	สวัสดี!	sà-wàt-dee
greeting (n)	คำทักทาย	kham thák thaai
to greet (vt)	ทักทาย	thák thaai
How are you? (form.)	คุณสบายดีไหม?	khun sà-baai dee măi
How are you? (fam.)	สบายดีไหม?	sà-baai dee măi
What's new?	มีอะไรใหม?	mee à-rai mài
Goodbye!	ลาก่อน!	laa gòrn
Bye!	บาย!	baai
See you soon!	พบกันใหม่	phóp gan mài
Farewell! (to a friend)	ลาก่อน!	laa gòrn
Farewell! (form.)	สวัสดี!	sà-wàt-dee
to say goodbye	บอกลา	bòrk laa
So long!	ลาก่อน!	laa gòrn
Thank you!	ขอบคุณ!	khòrp khun
Thank you very much!	ขอบคุณมาก!	khòrp khun mâak
You're welcome	ยินดีช่วย	yin dee chûay

Don't mention it!	ไม่เป็นไร	mâi bpen rai
It was nothing	ไม่เป็นไร	mâi bpen rai
Excuse me! (fam.)	ขอโทษที!	khŏr thôht thee
Excuse me! (form.)	ขอโทษ ครับ/ค่ะ!	khŏr thôht khráp / khâ
to excuse (forgive)	ให้อภัย	hâi a-phai
to apologize (vi)	ขอโทษ	khŏr thôht
My apologies	ขอโทษ	khŏr thôht
I'm sorry!	ขอโทษ!	khŏr thôht
to forgive (vt)	อภัย	a-phai
It's okay! (that's all right)	ไม่เป็นไร!	mâi bpen rai
please (adv)	โปรด	bpròht
Don't forget!	อย่าลืม!	yàa leum
Certainly!	แน่นอน!	nâe norn
Of course not!	ไม่ใช่แน่!	mâi châi nâe
Okay! (I agree)	โอเค!	oh-khay
That's enough!	พอแล้ว	phor láew

3. Questions

Who?	ใคร?	khrai
What?	อะไร?	a-rai
Where? (at, in)	ที่ไหน?	thêe năi
Where (to)?	ที่ไหน?	thêe năi
From where?	จากที่ไหน?	jàak thêe năi
When?	เมื่อไหร่?	mêua rài
Why? (What for?)	ทำไม?	tham-mai
Why? (~ are you crying?)	ทำไม?	tham-mai
What for?	เพื่ออะไร?	phêua a-rai
How? (in what way)	อย่างไร?	yàang rai
What? (What kind of ... ?)	อะไร?	a-rai
Which?	ไหน?	năi
To whom?	สำหรับใคร?	săm-ràp khrai
About whom?	เกี่ยวกับใคร?	gìeow gàp khrai
About what?	เกี่ยวกับอะไร?	gìeow gàp a-rai
With whom?	กับใคร?	gàp khrai
How many?	กี่...?	gèe...?
How much?	เท่าไหร่?	thâo rài
Whose?	ของใคร?	khŏrng khrai

4. Prepositions

with (accompanied by)	กับ	gàp
without	ปราศจาก	bpràat-sà-jàak

to (indicating direction)	ไปที่	bpai thêe
about (talking ~ …)	เกี่ยวกับ	gìeow gàp
before (in time)	ก่อน	gòrn
in front of …	หน้า	nâa
under (beneath, below)	ใต้	dtâi
above (over)	เหนือ	nĕua
on (atop)	บน	bon
from (off, out of)	จาก	jàak
of (made from)	ทำใช้	tham chái
in (e.g., ~ ten minutes)	ใน	nai
over (across the top of)	ขาม	khâam

5. Function words. Adverbs. Part 1

Where? (at, in)	ที่ไหน?	thêe nǎi
here (adv)	ที่นี่	thêe nêe
there (adv)	ที่นั่น	thêe nân
somewhere (to be)	ที่ใดที่หนึ่ง	thêe dai thêe nèung
nowhere (not in any place)	ไม่มีที่ไหน	mâi mee thêe nǎi
by (near, beside)	ข้าง	khâang
by the window	ขางหน้าต่าง	khâang nâa dtàang
Where (to)?	ที่ไหน?	thêe nǎi
here (e.g., come ~!)	ที่นี่	thêe nêe
there (e.g., to go ~)	ที่นั่น	thêe nân
from here (adv)	จากที่นี่	jàak thêe nêe
from there (adv)	จากที่นั่น	jàak thêe nân
close (adv)	ใกล้	glâi
far (adv)	ไกล	glai
near (e.g., ~ Paris)	ใกล้	glâi
nearby (adv)	ใกล้ๆ	glâi glâi
not far (adv)	ไม่ไกล	mâi glai
left (adj)	ซ้าย	sáai
on the left	ขางซ้าย	khâang sáai
to the left	ซ้าย	sáai
right (adj)	ขวา	khwǎa
on the right	ขางขวา	khâang khwǎa
to the right	ขวา	khwǎa
in front (adv)	ข้างหน้า	khâang nâa
front (as adj)	หน้า	nâa
ahead (the kids ran ~)	หน้า	nâa

behind (adv)	ข้างหลัง	khâang lăng
from behind	จากข้างหลัง	jàak khâang lăng
back (towards the rear)	หลัง	lăng

| middle | กลาง | glaang |
| in the middle | ตรงกลาง | dtrorng glaang |

at the side	ข้าง	khâang
everywhere (adv)	ทุกที่	thúk thêe
around (in all directions)	รอบ	rôrp

from inside	จากข้างใน	jàak khâang nai
somewhere (to go)	ที่ไหน	thêe năi
straight (directly)	ตรงไป	dtrorng bpai
back (e.g., come ~)	กลับ	glàp

| from anywhere | จากที่ใด | jàak thêe dai |
| from somewhere | จากที่ใด | jàak thêe dai |

firstly (adv)	ข้อที่หนึ่ง	khôr thêe nèung
secondly (adv)	ขอที่สอง	khôr thêe sŏrng
thirdly (adv)	ขอที่สาม	khôr thêe săam

suddenly (adv)	ในทันที	nai than thee
at first (in the beginning)	ตอนแรก	dtorn-râek
for the first time	เป็นครั้งแรก	bpen khráng râek
long before ...	นานก่อน	naan gòrn
anew (over again)	ใหม่	mài
for good (adv)	ให้จบสิ้น	hâi jòp sîn

never (adv)	ไม่เคย	mâi khoie
again (adv)	อีกครั้งหนึ่ง	èek khráng nèung
now (at present)	ตอนนี้	dtorn-née
often (adv)	บ่อย	bòi
then (adv)	เวลานั้น	way-laa nán
urgently (quickly)	อย่างเร่งด่วน	yàang râyng dùan
usually (adv)	มักจะ	mák jà

by the way, ...	อนึ่ง	à-nèung
possibly	เป็นไปได้	bpen bpai dâai
probably (adv)	อาจจะ	àat jà
maybe (adv)	อาจจะ	àat jà
besides ...	นอกจากนั้น...	nôrk jàak nán...
that's why ...	นั้นเป็นเหตุผลที่...	nân bpen hàyt phŏn thêe...
in spite of ...	แม้ว่า...	máe wâa...
thanks to ...	เนื่องจาก...	nêuang jàak...

what (pron.)	อะไร	a-rai
that (conj.)	ที่	thêe
something	อะไร	a-rai
anything (something)	อะไรก็ตาม	a-rai gôr dtaam
nothing	ไม่มีอะไร	mâi mee a-rai

who (pron.)	ใคร	khrai
someone	บางคน	baang khon
somebody	บางคน	baang khon
nobody	ไม่มีใคร	mâi mee khrai
nowhere (a voyage to ~)	ไม่ไปไหน	mâi bpai nǎi
nobody's	ไม่เป็นของของใคร	mâi bpen khǒrng khǒrng khrai
somebody's	ของคนหนึ่ง	khǒrng khon nèung
so (I'm ~ glad)	มาก	mâak
also (as well)	ด้วย	dûay
too (as well)	ด้วย	dûay

6. Function words. Adverbs. Part 2

Why?	ทำไม?	tham-mai
for some reason	เพราะเหตุผลอะไร	phrór hàyt phǒn à-rai
because ...	เพราะว่า...	phrór wâa
for some purpose	ด้วยจุดประสงค์อะไร	dûay jùt bprà-sǒng a-rai
and	และ	láe
or	หรือ	rěu
but	แต่	dtàe
for (e.g., ~ me)	สำหรับ	sǎm-ràp
too (~ many people)	เกินไป	gern bpai
only (exclusively)	เท่านั้น	thâo nán
exactly (adv)	ตรง	dtrorng
about (more or less)	ประมาณ	bprà-maan
approximately (adv)	ประมาณ	bprà-maan
approximate (adj)	ประมาณ	bprà-maan
almost (adv)	เกือบ	gèuap
the rest	ที่เหลือ	thêe lěua
the other (second)	อีก	èek
other (different)	อื่น	èun
each (adj)	ทุก	thúk
any (no matter which)	ใดๆ	dai dai
many (adj)	หลาย	lǎai
much (adv)	มาก	mâak
many people	หลายคน	lǎai khon
all (everyone)	ทุกๆ	thúk thúk
in return for ...	ที่จะเปลี่ยนเป็น	thêe jà bplìan bpen
in exchange (adv)	แทน	thaen
by hand (made)	ใช้มือ	chái meu
hardly (negative opinion)	แทบจะไม่	thâep jà mâi
probably (adv)	อาจจะ	àat jà

on purpose (intentionally)	โดยเจตนา	doi jàyt-dtà-naa
by accident (adv)	บังเอิญ	bang-ern
very (adv)	มาก	mâak
for example (adv)	ยกตัวอย่าง	yók dtua yàang
between	ระหว่าง	rá-wàang
among	ทามกลาง	tâam-glaang
so much (such a lot)	มากมาย	mâak maai
especially (adv)	โดยเฉพาะ	doi chà-phór

NUMBERS. MISCELLANEOUS

7. Cardinal numbers. Part 1

0 zero	ศูนย์	sŏon
1 one	หนึ่ง	nèung
2 two	สอง	sŏrng
3 three	สาม	săam
4 four	สี่	sèe

5 five	ห้า	hâa
6 six	หก	hòk
7 seven	เจ็ด	jèt
8 eight	แปด	bpàet
9 nine	เก้า	gâo

10 ten	สิบ	sìp
11 eleven	สิบเอ็ด	sìp èt
12 twelve	สิบสอง	sìp sŏrng
13 thirteen	สิบสาม	sìp săam
14 fourteen	สิบสี่	sìp sèe

15 fifteen	สิบห้า	sìp hâa
16 sixteen	สิบหก	sìp hòk
17 seventeen	สิบเจ็ด	sìp jèt
18 eighteen	สิบแปด	sìp bpàet
19 nineteen	สิบเก้า	sìp gâo

20 twenty	ยี่สิบ	yêe sìp
21 twenty-one	ยี่สิบเอ็ด	yêe sìp èt
22 twenty-two	ยี่สิบสอง	yêe sìp sŏrng
23 twenty-three	ยี่สิบสาม	yêe sìp săam

30 thirty	สามสิบ	săam sìp
31 thirty-one	สามสิบเอ็ด	săam-sìp-èt
32 thirty-two	สามสิบสอง	săam-sìp-sŏrng
33 thirty-three	สามสิบสาม	săam-sìp-săam

40 forty	สี่สิบ	sèe sìp
41 forty-one	สี่สิบเอ็ด	sèe-sìp-èt
42 forty-two	สี่สิบสอง	sèe-sìp-sŏrng
43 forty-three	สี่สิบสาม	sèe-sìp-săam

50 fifty	ห้าสิบ	hâa sìp
51 fifty-one	ห้าสิบเอ็ด	hâa-sìp-èt
52 fifty-two	หาสิบสอง	hâa-sìp-sŏrng

53 fifty-three	ห้าสิบสาม	hâa-sìp-sǎam
60 sixty	หกสิบ	hòk sìp
61 sixty-one	หกสิบเอ็ด	hòk-sìp-èt
62 sixty-two	หกสิบสอง	hòk-sìp-sǒrng
63 sixty-three	หกสิบสาม	hòk-sìp-sǎam

70 seventy	เจ็ดสิบ	jèt sìp
71 seventy-one	เจ็ดสิบเอ็ด	jèt-sìp-èt
72 seventy-two	เจ็ดสิบสอง	jèt-sìp-sǒrng
73 seventy-three	เจ็ดสิบสาม	jèt-sìp-sǎam

80 eighty	แปดสิบ	bpàet sìp
81 eighty-one	แปดสิบเอ็ด	bpàet-sìp-èt
82 eighty-two	แปดสิบสอง	bpàet-sìp-sǒrng
83 eighty-three	แปดสิบสาม	bpàet-sìp-sǎam

90 ninety	เก้าสิบ	gâo sìp
91 ninety-one	เก้าสิบเอ็ด	gâo-sìp-èt
92 ninety-two	เก้าสิบสอง	gâo-sìp-sǒrng
93 ninety-three	เกาสิบสาม	gâo-sìp-sǎam

8. Cardinal numbers. Part 2

100 one hundred	หนึ่งร้อย	nèung rói
200 two hundred	สองร้อย	sǒrng rói
300 three hundred	สามร้อย	sǎam rói
400 four hundred	สี่ร้อย	sèe rói
500 five hundred	ห้าร้อย	hâa rói

600 six hundred	หกร้อย	hòk rói
700 seven hundred	เจ็ดร้อย	jèt rói
800 eight hundred	แปดร้อย	bpàet rói
900 nine hundred	เก้าร้อย	gâo rói

1000 one thousand	หนึ่งพัน	nèung phan
2000 two thousand	สองพัน	sǒrng phan
3000 three thousand	สามพัน	sǎam phan
10000 ten thousand	หนึ่งหมื่น	nèung mèun
one hundred thousand	หนึ่งแสน	nèung sǎen
million	ลาน	láan
billion	พันลาน	phan láan

9. Ordinal numbers

first (adj)	แรก	râek
second (adj)	ที่สอง	thêe sǒrng
third (adj)	ที่สาม	thêe sǎam
fourth (adj)	ที่สี่	thêe sèe

fifth (adj)	ที่ห้า	thêe hâa
sixth (adj)	ที่หก	thêe hòk
seventh (adj)	ที่เจ็ด	thêe jèt
eighth (adj)	ที่แปด	thêe bpàet
ninth (adj)	ที่เก้า	thêe gâo
tenth (adj)	ที่สิบ	thêe sìp

COLOURS. UNITS OF MEASUREMENT

10. Colors

color	สี	sěe
shade (tint)	สีอ่อน	sěe òrn
hue	สีสัน	sěe săn
rainbow	สายรุ้ง	săai rúng
white (adj)	สีขาว	sěe khăao
black (adj)	สีดำ	sěe dam
gray (adj)	สีเทา	sěe thao
green (adj)	สีเขียว	sěe khĭeow
yellow (adj)	สีเหลือง	sěe lěuang
red (adj)	สีแดง	sěe daeng
blue (adj)	สีน้ำเงิน	sěe nám ngern
light blue (adj)	สีฟ้า	sěe fáa
pink (adj)	สีชมพู	sěe chom-poo
orange (adj)	สีส้ม	sěe sôm
violet (adj)	สีม่วง	sěe mûang
brown (adj)	สีน้ำตาล	sěe nám dtaan
golden (adj)	สีทอง	sěe thorng
silvery (adj)	สีเงิน	sěe ngern
beige (adj)	สีน้ำตาลอ่อน	sěe nám dtaan òrn
cream (adj)	สีครีม	sěe khreem
turquoise (adj)	สีเขียวแกม	sěe khĭeow gaem
	น้ำเงิน	náam ngern
cherry red (adj)	สีแดงเชอร์รี่	sěe daeng cher-rêe
lilac (adj)	สีม่วงอ่อน	sěe mûang-òrn
crimson (adj)	สีแดงเข้ม	sěe daeng khâym
light (adj)	อ่อน	òrn
dark (adj)	แก่	gàe
bright, vivid (adj)	สด	sòt
colored (pencils)	สี	sěe
color (e.g., ~ film)	สี	sěe
black-and-white (adj)	ขาวดำ	khăao-dam
plain (one-colored)	สีเดียว	sěe dieow
multicolored (adj)	หลากสี	làak sěe

11. Units of measurement

weight	น้ำหนัก	nám nàk
length	ความยาว	khwaam yaao
width	ความกว้าง	khwaam gwâang
height	ความสูง	khwaam sŏong
depth	ความลึก	khwaam léuk
volume	ปริมาณ	bpà-rí-maan
area	บริเวณ	bor-rí-wayn
gram	กรัม	gram
milligram	มิลลิกรัม	min-lí gram
kilogram	กิโลกรัม	gì-loh gram
ton	ตัน	dtan
pound	ปอนด์	bporn
ounce	ออนซ์	orn
meter	เมตร	máyt
millimeter	มิลลิเมตร	min-lí mâyt
centimeter	เซ็นติเมตร	sen dtì mâyt
kilometer	กิโลเมตร	gì-loh máyt
mile	ไมล์	mai
inch	นิ้ว	níw
foot	ฟุต	fút
yard	หลา	lăa
square meter	ตารางเมตร	dtaa-raang máyt
hectare	เฮกตาร์	hêek dtaa
liter	ลิตร	lít
degree	องศา	ong-săa
volt	โวลต์	wohn
ampere	แอมแปร์	aem-bpae
horsepower	แรงมา	raeng máa
quantity	จำนวน	jam-nuan
a little bit of ...	นิดนอย	nít nói
half	ครึ่ง	khrêung
dozen	โหล	lŏh
piece (item)	สวน	sùan
size	ขนาด	khà-nàat
scale (map ~)	มาตราส่วน	mâat-dtraa sùan
minimal (adj)	น้อยที่สุด	nói thêe sùt
the smallest (adj)	เล็กที่สุด	lék thêe sùt
medium (adj)	กลาง	glaang
maximal (adj)	สูงสุด	sŏong sùt
the largest (adj)	ใหญ่ที่สุด	yài têe sùt

12. Containers

canning jar (glass ~)	ขวดโหล	khùat lŏh
can	กระป๋อง	grà-bpŏrng
bucket	ถัง	thăng
barrel	ถัง	thăng
wash basin (e.g., plastic ~)	กะทะ	gà-thá
tank (100L water ~)	ถังเก็บน้ำ	thăng gèp nám
hip flask	กระติกน้ำ	grà-dtìk nám
jerrycan	ภาชนะ	phaa-chá-ná
tank (e.g., tank car)	ถังบรรจุ	thăng ban-jù
mug	แก้ว	gâew
cup (of coffee, etc.)	ถ้วย	thûay
saucer	จานรอง	jaan rorng
glass (tumbler)	แก้ว	gâew
wine glass	แก้วไวน์	gâew wai
stock pot (soup pot)	หม้อ	môr
bottle (~ of wine)	ขวด	khùat
neck (of the bottle, etc.)	ปาก	bpàak
carafe (decanter)	คนโท	khon-thoh
pitcher	เหยือก	yèuak
vessel (container)	ภาชนะ	phaa-chá-ná
pot (crock, stoneware ~)	หม้อ	môr
vase	แจกัน	jae-gan
flacon, bottle (perfume ~)	กระติก	grà-dtìk
vial, small bottle	ขวดเล็ก	khùat lék
tube (of toothpaste)	หลอด	lòrt
sack (bag)	ถุง	thŭng
bag (paper ~, plastic ~)	ถุง	thŭng
pack (of cigarettes, etc.)	ซอง	sorng
box (e.g., shoebox)	กล่อง	glòrng
crate	ลัง	lang
basket	ตะกร้า	dtà-grâa

MAIN VERBS

13. The most important verbs. Part 1

to advise (vt)	แนะนำ	náe nam
to agree (say yes)	เห็นด้วย	hĕn dûay
to answer (vi, vt)	ตอบ	dtòrp
to apologize (vi)	ขอโทษ	khŏr thôht
to arrive (vi)	มา	maa
to ask (~ oneself)	ถาม	thăam
to ask (~ sb to do sth)	ขอ	khŏr
to be (vi)	เป็น	bpen
to be afraid	กลัว	glua
to be hungry	หิว	hĭw
to be interested in ...	สนใจใน	sŏn jai nai
to be needed	ต้องการ	dtôrng gaan
to be surprised	ประหลาดใจ	bprà-làat jai
to be thirsty	กระหายน้ำ	grà-hăai náam
to begin (vt)	เริ่ม	rêrm
to belong to ...	เป็นของของ...	bpen khŏrng khŏrng...
to boast (vi)	โอ้อวด	ôh ùat
to break (split into pieces)	แตก	dtàek
to call (~ for help)	เรียก	rîak
can (v aux)	สามารถ	săa-mâat
to catch (vt)	จับ	jàp
to change (vt)	เปลี่ยน	bplìan
to choose (select)	เลือก	lêuak
to come down (the stairs)	ลง	long
to compare (vt)	เปรียบเทียบ	bpriap thîap
to complain (vi, vt)	บ่น	bòn
to confuse (mix up)	สับสน	sàp sŏn
to continue (vt)	ทำต่อไป	tham dtòr bpai
to control (vt)	ควบคุม	khûap khum
to cook (dinner)	ทำอาหาร	tham aa-hăan
to cost (vt)	ราคา	raa-khaa
to count (add up)	นับ	náp
to count on ...	พึ่งพา	phêung phaa
to create (vt)	สร้าง	sâang
to cry (weep)	ร้องไห้	rórng hâi

14. The most important verbs. Part 2

to deceive (vi, vt)	หลอก	lòrk
to decorate (tree, street)	ประดับ	bprà-dàp
to defend (a country, etc.)	ปกป้อง	bpòk bpôrng
to demand (request firmly)	เรียกร้อง	rîak rórng
to dig (vt)	ขุด	khùt
to discuss (vt)	หารือ	hǎa-reu
to do (vt)	ทำ	tham
to doubt (have doubts)	สงสัย	sǒng-sǎi
to drop (let fall)	ทิ้งให้ตก	thíng hâi dtòk
to enter	เขา	khâo
(room, house, etc.)		
to excuse (forgive)	ให้อภัย	hâi a-phai
to exist (vi)	มีอยู่	mee yòo
to expect (foresee)	คาดหวัง	khâat wǎng
to explain (vt)	อธิบาย	à-thí-baai
to fall (vi)	ตก	dtòk
to find (vt)	พบ	phóp
to finish (vt)	จบ	jòp
to fly (vi)	บิน	bin
to follow ... (come after)	ไปตาม...	bpai dtaam...
to forget (vi, vt)	ลืม	leum
to forgive (vt)	ให้อภัย	hâi a-phai
to give (vt)	ให้	hâi
to give a hint	บอกใบ้	bòrk bâi
to go (on foot)	ไป	bpai
to go for a swim	ไปว่ายน้ำ	bpai wâai náam
to go out (for dinner, etc.)	ออกไป	òrk bpai
to guess (the answer)	คาดเดา	khâat dao
to have (vt)	มี	mee
to have breakfast	ทานอาหารเช้า	thaan aa-hǎan cháo
to have dinner	ทานอาหารเย็น	thaan aa-hǎan yen
to have lunch	ทานอาหารเที่ยง	thaan aa-hǎan thîang
to hear (vt)	ได้ยิน	dâai yin
to help (vt)	ช่วย	chûay
to hide (vt)	ซ่อน	sôrn
to hope (vi, vt)	หวัง	wǎng
to hunt (vi, vt)	ล่า	lâa
to hurry (vi)	รีบ	rêep

15. The most important verbs. Part 3

to inform (vt)	แจ้ง	jâeng
to insist (vi, vt)	ยืนยัน	yeun yan
to insult (vt)	ดูถูก	doo thòok
to invite (vt)	เชิญ	chern
to joke (vi)	ล้อเล่น	lór lên
to keep (vt)	รักษา	rák-săa
to keep silent, to hush	นิ่งเงียบ	nîng ngîap
to kill (vt)	ฆ่า	khâa
to know (sb)	รู้จัก	róo jàk
to know (sth)	รู้	róo
to laugh (vi)	หัวเราะ	hŭa rór
to liberate (city, etc.)	ปลดปล่อย	bplòt bplòi
to like (I like …)	ชอบ	chôrp
to look for … (search)	หา	hăa
to love (sb)	รัก	rák
to make a mistake	ทำผิด	tham phìt
to manage, to run	บริหาร	bor-rí-hăan
to mean (signify)	หมาย	măai
to mention (talk about)	กล่าวถึง	glàao thĕung
to miss (school, etc.)	พลาด	phlâat
to notice (see)	สังเกต	săng-gàyt
to object (vi, vt)	ค้าน	kháan
to observe (see)	สังเกตการณ์	săng-gàyt gaan
to open (vt)	เปิด	bpèrt
to order (meal, etc.)	สั่ง	sàng
to order (mil.)	สั่งการ	sàng gaan
to own (possess)	เป็นเจ้าของ	bpen jâo khŏrng
to participate (vi)	มีส่วนร่วม	mee sùan rûam
to pay (vi, vt)	จ่าย	jàai
to permit (vt)	อนุญาต	a-nú-yâat
to plan (vt)	วางแผน	waang phăen
to play (children)	เล่น	lên
to pray (vi, vt)	ภาวนา	phaa-wá-naa
to prefer (vt)	ชอบ	chôrp
to promise (vt)	สัญญา	săn-yaa
to pronounce (vt)	ออกเสียง	òrk sĭang
to propose (vt)	เสนอ	sà-nĕr
to punish (vt)	ลงโทษ	long thôht

16. The most important verbs. Part 4

to read (vi, vt)	อ่าน	àan
to recommend (vt)	แนะนำ	náe nam

to refuse (vi, vt)	ปฏิเสธ	bpà-dtì-sàyt
to regret (be sorry)	เสียใจ	sĭa jai
to rent (sth from sb)	เชา	châo
to repeat (say again)	ซ้ำ	sám
to reserve, to book	จอง	jorng
to run (vi)	วิ่ง	wîng
to save (rescue)	กู้	gôo
to say (~ thank you)	บอก	bòrk
to scold (vt)	ดุด่า	dù dàa
to see (vt)	เห็น	hĕn
to sell (vt)	ขาย	khăai
to send (vt)	ส่ง	sòng
to shoot (vi)	ยิง	ying
to shout (vi)	ตะโกน	dtà-gohn
to show (vt)	แสดง	sà-daeng
to sign (document)	ลงนาม	long naam
to sit down (vi)	นั่ง	nâng
to smile (vi)	ยิ้ม	yím
to speak (vi, vt)	พูด	phôot
to steal (money, etc.)	ขโมย	khà-moi
to stop (for pause, etc.)	หยุด	yùt
to stop	หยุด	yùt
(please ~ calling me)		
to study (vt)	เรียน	rian
to swim (vi)	ว่ายน้ำ	wâai náam
to take (vt)	เอา	ao
to think (vi, vt)	คิด	khít
to threaten (vt)	ขู่	khòo
to touch (with hands)	แตะต้อง	dtàe dtôrng
to translate (vt)	แปล	bplae
to trust (vt)	เชื่อ	chêua
to try (attempt)	พยายาม	phá-yaa-yaam
to turn (e.g., ~ left)	เลี้ยว	líeow
to underestimate (vt)	ดูถูก	doo thòok
to understand (vt)	เข้าใจ	khâo jai
to unite (vt)	สมาน	sà-măan
to wait (vt)	รอ	ror
to want (wish, desire)	ต้องการ	dtôrng gaan
to warn (vt)	เตือน	dteuan
to work (vi)	ทำงาน	tham ngaan
to write (vt)	เขียน	khĭan
to write down	จด	jòt

TIME. CALENDAR

17. Weekdays

Monday	วันจันทร์	wan jan
Tuesday	วันอังคาร	wan ang-khaan
Wednesday	วันพุธ	wan phút
Thursday	วันพฤหัสบดี	wan phá-réu-hàt-sà-bor-dee
Friday	วันศุกร์	wan sùk
Saturday	วันเสาร์	wan săo
Sunday	วันอาทิตย์	wan aa-thít
today (adv)	วันนี้	wan née
tomorrow (adv)	พรุ่งนี้	phrûng-née
the day after tomorrow	วันมะรืนนี้	wan má-reun née
yesterday (adv)	เมื่อวานนี้	mêua waan née
the day before yesterday	เมื่อวานซืนนี้	mêua waan-seun née
day	วัน	wan
working day	วันทำงาน	wan tham ngaan
public holiday	วันนักขัตฤกษ์	wan nák-khàt-rêrk
day off	วันหยุด	wan yùt
weekend	วันสุดสัปดาห์	wan sùt sàp-daa
all day long	ทั้งวัน	tháng wan
the next day (adv)	วันรุ่งขึ้น	wan rûng khêun
two days ago	สองวันก่อน	sŏrng wan gòrn
the day before	วันก่อนหน้านี้	wan gòrn nâa née
daily (adj)	รายวัน	raai wan
every day (adv)	ทุกวัน	thúk wan
week	สัปดาห์	sàp-daa
last week (adv)	สัปดาห์ก่อน	sàp-daa gòrn
next week (adv)	สัปดาห์หน้า	sàp-daa nâa
weekly (adj)	รายสัปดาห์	raai sàp-daa
every week (adv)	ทุกสัปดาห์	thúk sàp-daa
twice a week	สัปดาห์ละสองครั้ง	sàp-daa lá sŏrng khráng
every Tuesday	ทุกวันอังคาร	túk wan ang-khaan

18. Hours. Day and night

morning	เช้า	cháo
in the morning	ตอนเช้า	dtorn cháo

| noon, midday | เที่ยงวัน | thîang wan |
| in the afternoon | ตอนบาย | dtorn bàai |

evening	เย็น	yen
in the evening	ตอนเย็น	dtorn yen
night	คืน	kheun
at night	กลางคืน	glaang kheun
midnight	เที่ยงคืน	thîang kheun

second	วินาที	wí-naa-thee
minute	นาที	naa-thee
hour	ชั่วโมง	chûa mohng
half an hour	ครึ่งชั่วโมง	khrêung chûa mohng
a quarter-hour	สิบห้านาที	sìp hâa naa-thee
fifteen minutes	สิบห้านาที	sìp hâa naa-thee
24 hours	24 ชั่วโมง	yêe sìp sèe · chûa mohng

sunrise	พระอาทิตย์ขึ้น	phrá aa-thít khêun
dawn	ใกล้รุ่ง	glâi rûng
early morning	เช้า	cháo
sunset	พระอาทิตย์ตก	phrá aa-thít dtòk

early in the morning	ตอนเช้า	dtorn cháo
this morning	เช้านี้	cháo née
tomorrow morning	พรุ่งนี้เช้า	phrûng-née cháo
this afternoon	บายนี้	bàai née
in the afternoon	ตอนบ่าย	dtorn bàai
tomorrow afternoon	พรุ่งนี้บาย	phrûng-née bàai

| tonight (this evening) | คืนนี้ | kheun née |
| tomorrow night | คืนพรุ่งนี้ | kheun phrûng-née |

at 3 o'clock sharp	3 โมงตรง	sǎam mohng dtrorng
about 4 o'clock	ประมาณ 4 โมง	bprà-maan sèe mohng
by 12 o'clock	ภายใน 12 โมง	phaai nai sìp sǒng mohng

in 20 minutes	อีก 20 นาที	èek yêe sìp naa-thee
in an hour	อีกหนึ่งชั่วโมง	èek nèung chûa mohng
on time (adv)	ทันเวลา	than way-laa

a quarter to ...	อีกสิบห้านาที	èek sìp hâa naa-thee
within an hour	ภายในหนึ่งชั่วโมง	phaai nai nèung chûa mohng
every 15 minutes	ทุก 15 นาที	thúk sìp hâa naa-thee
round the clock	ทั้งวัน	tháng wan

19. Months. Seasons

| January | มกราคม | mók-gà-raa khom |
| February | กุมภาพันธ์ | gum-phaa phan |

March	มีนาคม	mee-naa khom
April	เมษายน	may-sǎa-yon
May	พฤษภาคม	phréut-sà-phaa khom
June	มิถุนายน	mí-thù-naa-yon

July	กรกฎาคม	gà-rá-gà-daa-khom
August	สิงหาคม	sǐng hǎa khom
September	กันยายน	gan-yaa-yon
October	ตุลาคม	dtù-laa khom
November	พฤศจิกายน	phréut-sà-jì-gaa-yon
December	ธันวาคม	than-waa khom

spring	ฤดูใบไม้ผลิ	réu-doo bai máai phlì
in spring	ฤดูใบไม้ผลิ	réu-doo bai máai phlì
spring (as adj)	ฤดูใบไม้ผลิ	réu-doo bai máai phlì

summer	ฤดูร้อน	réu-doo rórn
in summer	ฤดูร้อน	réu-doo rórn
summer (as adj)	ฤดูรอน	réu-doo rórn

fall	ฤดูใบไม้ร่วง	réu-doo bai máai rûang
in fall	ฤดูใบไม้ร่วง	réu-doo bai máai rûang
fall (as adj)	ฤดูใบไมรวง	réu-doo bai máai rûang

winter	ฤดูหนาว	réu-doo nǎao
in winter	ฤดูหนาว	réu-doo nǎao
winter (as adj)	ฤดูหนาว	réu-doo nǎao

month	เดือน	deuan
this month	เดือนนี้	deuan née
next month	เดือนหน้า	deuan nâa
last month	เดือนที่แลว	deuan thêe láew

a month ago	หนึ่งเดือน กอนหนานี้	nèung deuan gòrn nâa née
in a month (a month later)	อีกหนึ่งเดือน	èek nèung deuan
in 2 months (2 months later)	อีกสองเดือน	èek sǒrng deuan
the whole month	ทั้งเดือน	tháng deuan
all month long	ตลอดทั้งเดือน	dtà-lòrt tháng deuan

monthly (~ magazine)	รายเดือน	raai deuan
monthly (adv)	ทุกเดือน	thúk deuan
every month	ทุกเดือน	thúk deuan
twice a month	เดือนละสองครั้ง	deuan lá sǒrng kráng

year	ปี	bpee
this year	ปีนี้	bpee née
next year	ปีหน้า	bpee nâa
last year	ปีที่แลว	bpee thêe láew
a year ago	หนึ่งปีกอน	nèung bpee gòrn
in a year	อีกหนึ่งปี	èek nèung bpee

in two years	อีกสองปี	èek sŏng bpee
the whole year	ทั้งปี	tháng bpee
all year long	ตลอดทั้งปี	dtà-lòrt tháng bpee
every year	ทุกปี	thúk bpee
annual (adj)	รายปี	raai bpee
annually (adv)	ทุกปี	thúk bpee
4 times a year	ปีละสี่ครั้ง	bpee lá sèe khráng
date (e.g., today's ~)	วันที่	wan thêe
date (e.g., ~ of birth)	วันเดือนปี	wan deuan bpee
calendar	ปฏิทิน	bpà-dtì-thin
half a year	ครึ่งปี	khrêung bpee
six months	หกเดือน	hòk deuan
season (summer, etc.)	ฤดูกาล	réu-doo gaan
century	ศตวรรษ	sà-dtà-wát

TRAVEL. HOTEL

20. Trip. Travel

tourism, travel	การท่องเที่ยว	gaan thôrng thîeow
tourist	นักท่องเที่ยว	nák thôrng thîeow
trip, voyage	การเดินทาง	gaan dern thaang
adventure	การผจญภัย	gaan phà-jon phai
trip, journey	การเดินทาง	gaan dern thaang
vacation	วันหยุดพักผ่อน	wan yùt phák phòrn
to be on vacation	หยุดพักผอน	yùt phák phòrn
rest	การพัก	gaan phák
train	รถไฟ	rót fai
by train	โดยรถไฟ	doi rót fai
airplane	เครื่องบิน	khrêuang bin
by airplane	โดยเครื่องบิน	doi khrêuang bin
by car	โดยรถยนต์	doi rót-yon
by ship	โดยเรือ	doi reua
luggage	สัมภาระ	săm-phaa-rá
suitcase	กระเป๋าเดินทาง	grà-bpǎo dern-thaang
luggage cart	รถขนสัมภาระ	rót khǒn săm-phaa-rá
passport	หนังสือเดินทาง	năng-sěu dern-thaang
visa	วีซา	wee-sâa
ticket	ตั๋ว	dtǔa
air ticket	ตั๋วเครื่องบิน	dtǔa khrêuang bin
guidebook	หนังสือแนะนำ	năng-sěu náe nam
map (tourist ~)	แผนที่	phǎen thêe
area (rural ~)	เขต	khàyt
place, site	สถานที่	sà-thǎan thêe
exotica (n)	สิ่งแปลกใหม่	sìng bplàek mài
exotic (adj)	ต่างแดน	dtàang daen
amazing (adj)	น่าประหลาดใจ	nâa bprà-làat jai
group	กลุ่ม	glùm
excursion, sightseeing tour	การเดินทาง ท่องเที่ยว	gaan dern taang thôrng thîeow
guide (person)	มัคคุเทศก์	mák-khú-thâyt

21. Hotel

hotel	โรงแรม	rohng raem
motel	โรงแรม	rohng raem
three-star (~ hotel)	สามดาว	sǎam daao
five-star	หาดาว	hâa daao
to stay (in a hotel, etc.)	พัก	phák
room	ห้อง	hôrng
single room	ห้องเดี่ยว	hôrng dìeow
double room	หองคู่	hôrng khôo
to book a room	จองหอง	jorng hôrng
half board	พักครึ่งวัน	phák khrêung wan
full board	พักเต็มวัน	phák dtem wan
with bath	มีห้องอาบน้ำ	mee hôrng àap náam
with shower	มีฝักบัว	mee fàk bua
satellite television	โทรทัศน์ดาวเทียม	thoh-rá-thát daao thiam
air-conditioner	เครื่องปรับอากาศ	khrêuang bpràp-aa-gàat
towel	ผ้าเช็ดตัว	phâa chét dtua
key	กุญแจ	gun-jae
administrator	นักบุริหาร	nák bor-rí-hǎan
chambermaid	แม่บ้าน	mâe bâan
porter, bellboy	พนักงาน ขนกระเป๋า	phá-nák ngaan khǒn grà-bpǎo
doorman	พนักงาน เปิดประตู	phá-nák ngaan bpèrt bprà-dtoo
restaurant	ร้านอาหาร	ráan aa-hǎan
pub, bar	บาร์	baa
breakfast	อาหารเช้า	aa-hǎan cháo
dinner	อาหารเย็น	aa-hǎan yen
buffet	บุฟเฟ่ต์	bùf-fây
lobby	ล็อบบี้	lórp-bêe
elevator	ลิฟต์	líf
DO NOT DISTURB	ห้ามรบกวน	hâam róp guan
NO SMOKING	หามสูบบุหรี่	hâam sòop bù rèe

22. Sightseeing

monument	อนุสาวรีย์	a-nú-sǎa-wá-ree
fortress	ป้อม	bpôrm
palace	วัง	wang
castle	ปราสาท	bpraa-sàat

tower	หอ	hǒr
mausoleum	สุสาน	sù-sǎan
architecture	สถาปัตยกรรม	sà-thǎa-bpàt-dtà-yá-gam
medieval (adj)	ยุคกลาง	yúk glaang
ancient (adj)	โบราณ	boh-raan
national (adj)	แห่งชาติ	hàeng châat
famous (monument, etc.)	ที่มีชื่อเสียง	thêe mee chêu-sǐang
tourist	นักท่องเที่ยว	nák thôrng thîeow
guide (person)	มัคคุเทศก์	mák-khú-thâyt
excursion, sightseeing tour	ทัศนศึกษา	thát-sà-ná-sèuk-sǎa
to show (vt)	แสดง	sà-daeng
to tell (vt)	เล่า	lâo
to find (vt)	หาพบ	hǎa phóp
to get lost (lose one's way)	หลงทาง	lǒng thaang
map (e.g., subway ~)	แผนที่	phǎen thêe
map (e.g., city ~)	แผนที่	phǎen thêe
souvenir, gift	ของที่ระลึก	khǒrng thêe rá-léuk
gift shop	ร้านขาย ของที่ระลึก	ráan khǎai khǒrng thêe rá-léuk
to take pictures	ถ่ายภาพ	thàai phâap
to have one's picture taken	ได้รับการ ถายภาพให	dâai ráp gaan thàai phâap hâi

TRANSPORTATION

23. Airport

airport	สนามบิน	sà-nǎam bin
airplane	เครื่องบิน	khrêuang bin
airline	สายการบิน	sǎai gaan bin
air traffic controller	เจ้าหน้าที่ควบคุม จราจรทางอากาศ	jâo nâa-thêe khûap khum jà-raa-jon thaang aa-gàat
departure	การออกเดินทาง	gaan òrk dern thaang
arrival	การมาถึง	gaan maa thěung
to arrive (by plane)	มาถึง	maa thěung
departure time	เวลาขาไป	way-laa khǎa bpai
arrival time	เวลามาถึง	way-laa maa thěung
to be delayed	ถูกเลื่อน	thòok lêuan
flight delay	เลื่อนเที่ยวบิน	lêuan thieow bin
information board	กระดานแสดง ข้อมูล	grà daan sà-daeng khôr moon
information	ข้อมูล	khôr moon
to announce (vt)	ประกาศ	bprà-gàat
flight (e.g., next ~)	เที่ยวบิน	thîeow bin
customs	ศุลกากร	sǔn-lá-gaa-gon
customs officer	เจ้าหน้าที่ ศุลกากร	jâo nâa-thêe sǔn-lá-gaa-gon
customs declaration	แบบฟอร์มการเสีย ภาษีศุลกากร	bàep form gaan sǐa phaa-sěe sǔn-lá-gaa-gon
to fill out (vt)	กรอก	gròrk
to fill out the declaration	กรอกแบบฟอร์ม การเสียภาษี	gròrk bàep form gaan sǐa paa-sěe
passport control	จุดตรวจหนังสือ เดินทาง	jùt dtrùat nǎng-sěu dern-thaang
luggage	สัมภาระ	sǎm-phaa-rá
hand luggage	กระเป๋าถือ	grà-bpǎo thěu
luggage cart	รถขนสัมภาระ	rót khǒn sǎm-phaa-rá
landing	การลงจอด	gaan long jòrt
landing strip	ลานบินลงจอด	laan bin long jòrt
to land (vi)	ลงจอด	long jòrt
airstair (passenger stair)	ทางขึ้นลง เครื่องบิน	thaang khêun long khrêuang bin

check-in	การเช็คอิน	gaan chék in
check-in counter	เคาน์เตอร์เช็คอิน	khao-dtêr chék in
to check-in (vi)	เช็คอิน	chék in
boarding pass	บัตรที่นั่ง	bàt thêe nâng
departure gate	ช่องเขา	chôrng khâo
transit	การต่อเที่ยวบิน	gaan tòr thîeow bin
to wait (vt)	รอ	ror
departure lounge	ห้องผู้โดยสาร ขาออก	hôrng phôo doi săan khăa òk
to see off	ไปส่ง	bpai sòng
to say goodbye	บอกลา	bòrk laa

24. Airplane

airplane	เครื่องบิน	khrêuang bin
air ticket	ตั๋วเครื่องบิน	dtŭa khrêuang bin
airline	สายการบิน	săai gaan bin
airport	สนามบิน	sà-năam bin
supersonic (adj)	ความเร็วเหนือเสียง	khwaam reo nĕua-sĭang
captain	กัปตัน	gàp dtan
crew	ลูกเรือ	lôok reua
pilot	นักบิน	nák bin
flight attendant (fem.)	พนักงานต้อนรับ บนเครื่องบิน	phá-nák ngaan dtôrn ráp bon khrêuang bin
navigator	ต้นหน	dtôn hŏn
wings	ปีก	bpèek
tail	หาง	hăang
cockpit	ห้องนักบิน	hôrng nák bin
engine	เครื่องยนต์	khrêuang yon
undercarriage (landing gear)	โครงส่วนล่าง ของเครื่องบิน	khrorng sùan lâang khŏrng khrêuang bin
turbine	กังหัน	gang-hăn
propeller	ใบพัด	bai phát
black box	กล่องดำ	glòrng dam
yoke (control column)	คันบังคับ	khan bang-kháp
fuel	เชื้อเพลิง	chéua phlerng
safety card	คู่มือความ ปลอดภัย	khôo meu khwaam bplòt phai
oxygen mask	หน้ากากอ็อกซิเจน	nâa gàak ók sí jayn
uniform	เครื่องแบบ	khrêuang bàep
life vest	เสื้อชูชีพ	sêua choo chêep
parachute	ร่มชูชีพ	rôm choo chêep
takeoff	การบินขึ้น	gaan bin khêun
to take off (vi)	บินขึ้น	bin khêun

runway	ทางวิ่งเครื่องบิน	thaang wîng khrêuang bin
visibility	ทัศนวิสัย	thát sá ná wí-săi
flight (act of flying)	การบิน	gaan bin
altitude	ความสูง	khwaam sŏong
air pocket	หลุมอากาศ	lŭm aa-gàat
seat	ที่นั่ง	thêe nâng
headphones	หูฟัง	hŏo fang
folding tray (tray table)	ถาดพับเก็บได้	thàat pháp gèp dâai
airplane window	หน้าต่างเครื่องบิน	nâa dtàang khrêuang bin
aisle	ทางเดิน	thaang dern

25. Train

train	รถไฟ	rót fai
commuter train	รถไฟชานเมือง	rót fai chaan meuang
express train	รถไฟด่วน	rót fai dùan
diesel locomotive	รถจักรดีเซล	rót jàk dee-sayn
steam locomotive	รถจักรไอน้ำ	rót jàk ai náam
passenger car	ตู้โดยสาร	dtôo doi săan
dining car	ตูเสบียง	dtôo sà-biang
rails	รางรถไฟ	raang rót fai
railroad	ทางรถไฟ	thaang rót fai
railway tie	หมอนรองราง	mŏrn rorng raang
platform (railway ~)	ชานชลา	chaan-chá-laa
track (~ 1, 2, etc.)	ราง	raang
semaphore	ไฟสัญญาณรถไฟ	fai săn-yaan rót fai
station	สถานี	sà-thăa-nee
engineer (train driver)	คนขับรถไฟ	khon khàp rót fai
porter (of luggage)	พนักงาน ยกกระเป๋า	phá-nák ngaan yók grà-bpăo
car attendant	พนักงานรถไฟ	phá-nák ngaan rót fai
passenger	ผู้โดยสาร	phôo doi săan
conductor (ticket inspector)	พนักงานตรวจตั๋ว	phá-nák ngaan dtrùat dtŭa
corridor (in train)	ทางเดิน	thaang dern
emergency brake	เบรคฉุกเฉิน	bràyk chùk-chĕrn
compartment	ตู้นอน	dtôo norn
berth	เตียง	dtiang
upper berth	เตียงบน	dtiang bon
lower berth	เตียงล่าง	dtiang lâang
bed linen, bedding	ชุดเครื่องนอน	chút khrêuang norn
ticket	ตั๋ว	dtŭa
schedule	ตารางเวลา	dtaa-raang way-laa

information display	ฉระดานแสดงข้อมูล	grà daan sà-daeng khôr moon
to leave, to depart	ออกเดินทาง	òrk dern thaang
departure (of train)	การออกเดินทาง	gaan òrk dern thaang
to arrive (ab. train)	มาถึง	maa thĕung
arrival	การมาถึง	gaan maa thĕung
to arrive by train	มาถึงโดยรถไฟ	maa thĕung doi rót fai
to get on the train	ขึ้นรถไฟ	khêun rót fai
to get off the train	ลงจากรถไฟ	long jàak rót fai
train wreck	รถไฟตกราง	rót fai dtòk raang
to derail (vi)	ตกราง	dtòk raang
steam locomotive	หัวรถจักรไอน้ำ	hŭa rót jàk ai náam
stoker, fireman	คนควบคุมเตาไฟ	khon khûap khum dtao fai
firebox	เตาไฟ	dtao fai
coal	ถานหิน	thàan hĭn

26. Ship

ship	เรือ	reua
vessel	เรือ	reua
steamship	เรือจักรไอน้ำ	reua jàk ai náam
riverboat	เรือลองแมน้ำ	reua lông mâe náam
cruise ship	เรือเดินสมุทร	reua dern sà-mùt
cruiser	เรือลาดตระเวน	reua lâat dtrà-wayn
yacht	เรือยอชต์	reua yôt
tugboat	เรือลากจูง	reua lâak joong
barge	เรือบูรรทุก	reua ban-thúk
ferry	เรือข้ามฟาก	reua khâam fâak
sailing ship	เรือใบ	reua bai
brigantine	เรือใบสองเสากระโดง	reua bai sŏrng săo grà-dohng
ice breaker	เรือตัดน้ำแข็ง	reua dtàt náam khăeng
submarine	เรือดำน้ำ	reua dam náam
boat (flat-bottomed ~)	เรือพาย	reua phaai
dinghy	เรือบดเล็ก	reua bòt lék
lifeboat	เรือชูชีพ	reua choo chêep
motorboat	เรือยนต์	reua yon
captain	กัปตัน	gàp dtan
seaman	นาวิน	naa-win
sailor	คนเรือ	khon reua
crew	กะลาสี	gà-laa-sĕe

boatswain	สรั่ง	sà-ràng
ship's boy	คนช่วยงาน ในเรือ	khon chûay ngaan nai reua
cook	กุ๊ก	gúk
ship's doctor	แพทย์เรือ	phâet reua
deck	ดาดฟ้าเรือ	dàat-fáa reua
mast	เสากระโดงเรือ	sǎo grà-dohng reua
sail	ใบเรือ	bai reua
hold	ท้องเรือ	thórng-reua
bow (prow)	หัวเรือ	hǔa-reua
stern	ท้ายเรือ	tháai reua
oar	ไม้พาย	máai phaai
screw propeller	ใบจักร	bai jàk
cabin	ห้องพัก	hôrng phák
wardroom	ห้องอาหาร	hôrng aa-hǎan
engine room	ห้องเครื่องยนต์	hôrng khrêuang yon
bridge	สะพานเดินเรือ	sà-phaan dern reua
radio room	ห้องวิทยุ	hôrng wít-thá-yú
wave (radio)	คลื่นความถี่	khlêun khwaam thèe
logbook	สมุดบันทึก	sà-mùt ban-théuk
spyglass	กล้องส่องทางไกล	glôrng sòrng thaang glai
bell	ระฆัง	rá-khang
flag	ธง	thorng
hawser (mooring ~)	เชือก	chêuak
knot (bowline, etc.)	ปม	bpom
deckrails	ราว	raao
gangway	ไม้พาดให้ ขึ้นลงเรือ	máai phâat hâi khêun long reua
anchor	สมอ	sà-mǒr
to weigh anchor	ถอนสมอ	thǒrn sà-mǒr
to drop anchor	ทอดสมอ	thôrt sà-mǒr
anchor chain	โซ่สมอเรือ	sôh sà-mǒr reua
port (harbor)	ท่าเรือ	thâa reua
quay, wharf	ท่า	thâa
to berth (moor)	จอดเทียบท่า	jòt thîap tâa
to cast off	ออกจากท่า	òrk jàak tâa
trip, voyage	การเดินทาง	gaan dern thaang
cruise (sea trip)	การล่องเรือ	gaan lôrng reua
course (route)	เส้นทาง	sên thaang
route (itinerary)	เส้นทาง	sên thaang

fairway (safe water channel)	ร่องเรือเดิน	rông reua dern
shallows	โขด	khòht
to run aground	เกยตื้น	goie dtêun

storm	พายุ	phaa-yú
signal	สัญญาณ	săn-yaan
to sink (vi)	ลม	lôm
Man overboard!	คนตกเรือ!	kon dtòk reua
SOS (distress signal)	SOS	es-o-es
ring buoy	ห่วงยาง	hùang yaang

CITY

27. Urban transportation

bus	รถเมล์	rót may
streetcar	รถราง	rót raang
trolley bus	รถโดยสารประจำ ทางไฟฟ้า	rót doi săan bprà-jam thaang fai fáa
route (of bus, etc.)	เส้นทาง	sên thaang
number (e.g., bus ~)	หมายเลข	măai lâyk
to go by ...	ไปด้วย	bpai dûay
to get on (~ the bus)	ขึ้น	khêun
to get off ...	ลง	long
stop (e.g., bus ~)	ป้าย	bpâai
next stop	ป้ายถัดไป	bpâai thàt bpai
terminus	ป้ายสุดท้าย	bpâai sùt tháai
schedule	ตารางเวลา	dtaa-raang way-laa
to wait (vt)	รอ	ror
ticket	ตั๋ว	dtŭa
fare	ค่าตั๋ว	khâa dtŭa
cashier (ticket seller)	คนขายตั๋ว	khon khăai dtŭa
ticket inspection	การตรวจตั๋ว	gaan dtrùat dtŭa
ticket inspector	พนักงานตรวจตั๋ว	phá-nák ngaan dtrùat dtŭa
to be late (for ...)	ไปสาย	bpai săai
to miss (~ the train, etc.)	พลาด	phlâat
to be in a hurry	รีบเร่ง	rêep râyng
taxi, cab	แท็กซี่	tháek-sêe
taxi driver	คนขับแท็กซี่	khon khàp tháek-sêe
by taxi	โดยแท็กซี่	doi tháek-sêe
taxi stand	ป้ายจอดแท็กซี่	bpâai jòrt tháek sêe
to call a taxi	เรียกแท็กซี่	rîak tháek sêe
to take a taxi	ขึ้นรถแท็กซี่	khêun rót tháek-sêe
traffic	การจราจร	gaan jà-raa-jon
traffic jam	การจราจรติดขัด	gaan jà-raa-jon dtìt khàt
rush hour	ชั่วโมงเร่งด่วน	chûa mohng râyng dùan
to park (vi)	จอด	jòrt
to park (vt)	จอด	jòrt
parking lot	ลานจอดรถ	laan jòrt rót
subway	รถไฟใต้ดิน	rót fai dtâi din

station	สถานี	sà-thǎa-nee
to take the subway	ขึ้นรถไฟใต้ดิน	khêun rót fai dtâi din
train	รถไฟ	rót fai
train station	สถานีรถไฟ	sà-thǎa-nee rót fai

28. City. Life in the city

city, town	เมือง	meuang
capital city	เมืองหลวง	meuang lǔang
village	หมู่บ้าน	mòo bâan

city map	แผนที่เมือง	phǎen thêe meuang
downtown	ใจกลางเมือง	jai glaang-meuang
suburb	ชานเมือง	chaan meuang
suburban (adj)	ชานเมือง	chaan meuang

outskirts	รอบนอกเมือง	rôrp nôrk meuang
environs (suburbs)	เขตรอบเมือง	khàyt rôrp-meuang
city block	บล็อกผังเมือง	blòrk phǎng meuang
residential block (area)	บล็อกที่อยู่อาศัย	blòrk thêe yòo aa-sǎi

traffic	การจราจร	gaan jà-raa-jon
traffic lights	ไฟจราจร	fai jà-raa-jon
public transportation	ขนส่งมวลชน	khǒn sòng muan chon
intersection	สี่แยก	sèe yâek

crosswalk	ทางม้าลาย	thaang máa laai
pedestrian underpass	อุโมงค์คนเดิน	u-mohng kon dern
to cross (~ the street)	ข้าม	khâam
pedestrian	คนเดินเท้า	khon dern tháo
sidewalk	ทางเท้า	thaang tháo

bridge	สะพาน	sà-phaan
embankment (river walk)	ทางเลียบแม่น้ำ	thaang lîap mâe náam
fountain	น้ำพุ	nám phú

allée (garden walkway)	ทางเลียบสวน	thaang lîap sǔan
park	สวน	sǔan
boulevard	ถนนกว้าง	thà-nǒn gwâang
square	จัตุรัส	jàt-dtù-ràt
avenue (wide street)	ถนนใหญ่	thà-nǒn yài
street	ถนน	thà-nǒn
side street	ซอย	soi
dead end	ทางตัน	thaang dtan

house	บ้าน	bâan
building	อาคาร	aa-khaan
skyscraper	ตึกระฟ้า	dtèuk rá-fáa
facade	ด้านหน้าอาคาร	dâan-nâa aa-khaan
roof	หลังคา	lǎng khaa

window	หูน้าต่าง	nâa dtàang
arch	ชุมประตู	súm bprà-dtoo
column	เสา	sǎo
corner	มุม	mum

store window	หูน้าต่างร้านค้า	nâa dtàang ráan kháa
signboard (store sign, etc.)	ป้ายราน	bpâai ráan
poster (e.g., playbill)	โปสเตอร์	bpòht-dtêr
advertising poster	ป้ายโฆษณา	bpâai khôht-sà-naa
billboard	กระดานปิดประกาศ โฆษณา	grà-daan bpìt bprà-gàat khôht-sà-naa

garbage, trash	ขยะ	khà-yà
trash can (public ~)	ถังขยะ	thǎng khà-yà
to litter (vi)	ทิ้งขยะ	thíng khà-yà
garbage dump	ที่ทิ้งขยะ	thêe thíng khà-yà

phone booth	ตู้โทรศัพท์	dtôo thoh-rá-sàp
lamppost	เสาโคม	sǎo khohm
bench (park ~)	มานั่ง	máa nâng

police officer	เจ้าหน้าที่ตำรวจ	jâo nâa-thêe dtam-rùat
police	ตำรวจ	dtam-rùat
beggar	ขอทาน	khǒr thaan
homeless (n)	คนไร้บาน	khon rái bâan

29. Urban institutions

store	ร้านค้า	ráan kháa
drugstore, pharmacy	ร้านขายยา	ráan khǎai yaa
eyeglass store	รานตัดแว่น	ráan dtàt wâen
shopping mall	ศูนย์การค้า	sǒon gaan kháa
supermarket	ซูเปอร์มาร์เก็ต	soo-bper-maa-gèt

bakery	ร้านขนมปัง	ráan khà-nǒm bpang
baker	คนอบขนมปัง	khon òp khà-nǒm bpang
pastry shop	ร้านขนม	ráan khà-nǒm
grocery store	ร้านขายของชำ	ráan khǎai khǒrng cham
butcher shop	รานขายเนื้อ	ráan khǎai néua

| produce store | ร้านขายผัก | ráan khǎai phàk |
| market | ตลาด | dtà-làat |

coffee house	ร้านกาแฟ	ráan gaa-fae
restaurant	รานอาหาร	ráan aa-hǎan
pub, bar	บาร์	baa
pizzeria	รานพิซซ่า	ráan phís-sâa

| hair salon | ร้านทำผม | ráan tham phǒm |
| post office | โรงไปรษณีย์ | rohng bprai-sà-nee |

dry cleaners	ร้านซักแห้ง	ráan sák hâeng
photo studio	ห้องถ่ายภาพ	hôrng thàai phâap
shoe store	ร้านขายรองเท้า	ráan khǎai rorng táo
bookstore	ร้านขายหนังสือ	ráan khǎai nǎng-sěu
sporting goods store	ร้านขายอุปกรณ์กีฬา	ráan khǎai u-bpà-gon gee-laa
clothes repair shop	ร้านซ่อมเสื้อผ้า	ráan sôrm sêua phâa
formal wear rental	ร้านเช่าเสื้อออกงาน	ráan châo sêua òrk ngaan
video rental store	ร้านเช่าวิดีโอ	ráan châo wí-dee-oh
circus	โรงละครสัตว์	rohng lá-khon sàt
zoo	สวนสัตว์	sǔan sàt
movie theater	โรงภาพยนตร์	rohng phâap-phá-yon
museum	พิพิธภัณฑ์	phí-phítha phan
library	ห้องสมุด	hôrng sà-mùt
theater	โรงละคร	rohng lá-khon
opera (opera house)	โรงอุปรากร	rohng ù-bpà-raa-gon
nightclub	ไนท์คลับ	nai-khláp
casino	คาสิโน	khaa-sì-noh
mosque	สุเหร่า	sù-rào
synagogue	โบสถ์ยิว	bòht yiw
cathedral	อาสนวิหาร	aa sǒn wí-hǎan
temple	วิหาร	wí-hǎan
church	โบสถ์	bòht
college	วิทยาลัย	wít-thá-yaa-lai
university	มหาวิทยาลัย	má-hǎa wít-thá-yaa-lai
school	โรงเรียน	rohng rian
prefecture	ศาลากลางจังหวัด	sǎa-laa glaang jang-wàt
city hall	ศาลาเทศบาล	sǎa-laa thâyt-sà-baan
hotel	โรงแรม	rohng raem
bank	ธนาคาร	thá-naa-khaan
embassy	สถานทูต	sà-thǎan thôot
travel agency	บริษัททัวร์	bor-rí-sàt thua
information office	สำนักงานศูนย์ข้อมูล	sǎm-nák ngaan sǒon khôr moon
currency exchange	ร้านแลกเงิน	ráan lâek ngern
subway	รถไฟใต้ดิน	rót fai dtâi din
hospital	โรงพยาบาล	rohng phá-yaa-baan
gas station	ปั๊มน้ำมัน	bpám náam man
parking lot	ลานจอดรถ	laan jòrt rót

30. Signs

signboard (store sign, etc.)	ป้ายร้าน	bpâai ráan
notice (door sign, etc.)	ป้ายเตือน	bpâai dteuan
poster	โปสเตอร์	bpòht-dtêr
direction sign	ป้ายบอกทาง	bpâai bòrk thaang
arrow (sign)	ลูกศร	lôok sŏn
caution	คำเตือน	kham dteuan
warning sign	ป้ายเตือน	bpâai dteuan
to warn (vt)	เตือน	dteuan
rest day (weekly ~)	วันหยุด	wan yùt
timetable (schedule)	ตารางเวลา	dtaa-raang way-laa
opening hours	เวลาทำการ	way-laa tham gaan
WELCOME!	ยินดีต้อนรับ!	yin dee dtôrn ráp
ENTRANCE	ทางเขา	thaang khâo
EXIT	ทางออก	thaang òrk
PUSH	ผลัก	phlàk
PULL	ดึง	deung
OPEN	เปิด	bpèrt
CLOSED	ปิด	bpìt
WOMEN	หญิง	yĭng
MEN	ชาย	chaai
DISCOUNTS	ลดราคา	lót raa-khaa
SALE	ขายของลดราคา	khăai khŏrng lót raa-khaa
NEW!	ใหม่!	mài
FREE	ฟรี	free
ATTENTION!	โปรดทราบ!	bpròht sâap
NO VACANCIES	ไม่มีห้องว่าง	mâi mee hôrng wâang
RESERVED	จองแลว	jorng láew
ADMINISTRATION	สำนักงาน	săm-nák ngaan
STAFF ONLY	เฉพาะพนักงาน	chà-phór phá-nák ngaan
BEWARE OF THE DOG!	ระวังสุนัข!	rá-wang sù-nák
NO SMOKING	ห้ามสูบบุหรี่	hâam sòop bù rèe
DO NOT TOUCH!	ห้ามแตะ!	hâam dtàe
DANGEROUS	อันตราย	an-dtà-raai
DANGER	อันตราย	an-dtà-raai
HIGH VOLTAGE	ไฟฟ้าแรงสูง	fai fáa raeng sŏong
NO SWIMMING!	ห้ามว่ายน้ำ!	hâam wâai náam
OUT OF ORDER	เสีย	sĭa
FLAMMABLE	อันตรายติดไฟ	an-dtà-raai dtìt fai
FORBIDDEN	ห้าม	hâam

| NO TRESPASSING! | ห้ามผ่าน! | hâam phàan |
| WET PAINT | สีพื้นเปียก | sěe phéun bpìak |

31. Shopping

to buy (purchase)	ซื้อ	séu
purchase	ของซื้อ	khǒrng séu
to go shopping	ไปซื้อของ	bpai séu khǒrng
shopping	การชอปปิง	gaan chôp bping

| to be open (ab. store) | เปิด | bpèrt |
| to be closed | ปิด | bpìt |

footwear, shoes	รองเท้า	rorng tháo
clothes, clothing	เสื้อผ้า	sêua phâa
cosmetics	เครื่องสำอาง	khrêuang sǎm-aang
food products	อาหาร	aa-hǎan
gift, present	ของขวัญ	khǒrng khwǎn

| salesman | พนักงานขาย | phá-nák ngaan khǎai |
| saleswoman | พนักงานขาย | phá-nák ngaan khǎai |

check out, cash desk	ที่จ่ายเงิน	thêe jàai ngern
mirror	กระจก	grà-jòk
counter (store ~)	เคาน์เตอร์	khao-dtêr
fitting room	ห้องลองเสื้อผ้า	hôrng lorng sêua phâa

to try on	ลอง	lorng
to fit (ab. dress, etc.)	เหมาะ	mò
to like (I like …)	ชอบ	chôrp

price	ราคา	raa-khaa
price tag	ป้ายราคา	bpâai raa-khaa
to cost (vt)	ราคา	raa-khaa
How much?	ราคาเท่าไหร่?	raa-khaa thâo rài
discount	ลดราคา	lót raa-khaa

inexpensive (adj)	ไม่แพง	mâi phaeng
cheap (adj)	ถูก	thòok
expensive (adj)	แพง	phaeng
It's expensive	มันราคาแพง	man raa-khaa phaeng

rental (n)	การเช่า	gaan châo
to rent (~ a tuxedo)	เช่า	châo
credit (trade credit)	สินเชื่อ	sǐn chêua
on credit (adv)	ซื้อเงินเชื่อ	séu ngern chêua

CLOTHING & ACCESSORIES

32. Outerwear. Coats

clothes	เสื้อผ้า	sêua phâa
outerwear	เสื้อนอก	sêua nôk
winter clothing	เสื้อกันหนาว	sêua gan năao
coat (overcoat)	เสื้อโค้ท	sêua khóht
fur coat	เสื้อโค้ทขนสัตว์	sêua khóht khŏn sàt
fur jacket	แจ็คเก็ตขนสัตว์	jáek-gèt khŏn sàt
down coat	แจ็คเก็ตกันหนาว	jáek-gèt gan năao
jacket (e.g., leather ~)	แจ๊คเก็ต	jáek-gèt
raincoat (trenchcoat, etc.)	เสื้อกันฝน	sêua gan fŏn
waterproof (adj)	ซึ่งกันน้ำได้	sêung gan náam dâai

33. Men's & women's clothing

shirt (button shirt)	เสื้อ	sêua
pants	กางเกง	gaang-gayng
jeans	กางเกงยีนส์	gaang-gayng yeen
suit jacket	แจ็คเก็ตสูท	jàek-gèt sòot
suit	ชุดสูท	chút sòot
dress (frock)	ชุดเดรส	chút draet
skirt	กระโปรง	grà bprohng
blouse	เสื้อ	sêua
knitted jacket (cardigan, etc.)	แจ็คเก็ตถัก	jáek-gèt thàk
jacket (of woman's suit)	แจ๊คเก็ต	jáek-gèt
T-shirt	เสื้อยืด	sêua yêut
shorts (short trousers)	กางเกงขาสั้น	gaang-gayng khăa sân
tracksuit	ชุดวอรม	chút wom
bathrobe	เสื้อคลุมอาบน้ำ	sêua khlum àap náam
pajamas	ชุดนอน	chút norn
sweater	เสื้อไหมพรม	sêua măi phrom
pullover	เสื้อกันหนาวแบบสวม	sêua gan năao bàep sŭam
vest	เสื้อกั๊ก	sêua gák
tailcoat	เสื้อเทลโค้ต	sêua thayn-khóht
tuxedo	ชุดทักซิโด	chút thák sí dôh

uniform	เครื่องแบบ	khrêuang bàep
workwear	ชุดทำงาน	chút tam ngaan
overalls	ชุดเอี๊ยม	chút íam
coat (e.g., doctor's smock)	เสื้อคลุม	sêua khlum

34. Clothing. Underwear

underwear	ชุดชั้นใน	chút chán nai
boxers, briefs	กางเกงในชาย	gaang-gayng nai chaai
panties	กางเกงในสตรี	gaang-gayng nai sàt-dtree
undershirt (A-shirt)	เสื้อชั้นใน	sêua chán nai
socks	ถุงเท้า	thǔng tháo

nightdress	ชุดนอนสตรี	chút norn sàt-dtree
bra	ยกทรง	yók song
knee highs (knee-high socks)	ถุงเท้ายาว	thǔng tháo yaao
pantyhose	ถุงน่องเต็มตัว	thǔng nôrng dtem dtua
stockings (thigh highs)	ถุงน่อง	thǔng nôrng
bathing suit	ชุดว่ายน้ำ	chút wâai náam

35. Headwear

hat	หมวก	mùak
fedora	หมวก	mùak
baseball cap	หมวกเบสบอล	mùak bàyt-bon
flatcap	หมวกติงลี่	mùak dting lêe

beret	หูมวกเบเร่ต์	mùak bay-rây
hood	ฮูด	hóot
panama hat	หมวกปานามา	mùak bpaa-naa-maa
knit cap (knitted hat)	หมวกไหมพรม	mùak mǎi phrom

headscarf	ผ้าโพกศีรษะ	phâa phôhk sěe-sà
women's hat	หมวกสตรี	mùak sàt-dtree
hard hat	หมวกนิรภัย	mùak ní-rá-phai
garrison cap	หมวกหนีบ	mùak nèep
helmet	หมวกกันน็อค	mùak ní-rá-phai

derby	หมวกกลมทรงสูง	mùak glom song sǒong
top hat	หมวกทรงสูง	mùak song sǒong

36. Footwear

footwear	รองเท้า	rorng tháo
shoes (men's shoes)	รองเท้า	rorng tháo

shoes (women's shoes)	รองเท้า	rorng tháo
boots (e.g., cowboy ~)	รองเท้าบูท	rorng tháo bòot
slippers	รองเท้าแตะในบ้าน	rorng tháo dtàe nai bâan
tennis shoes (e.g., Nike ~)	รองเท้ากีฬา	rorng tháo gee-laa
sneakers	รองเท้าผ้าใบ	rorng tháo phâa bai
(e.g., Converse ~)		
sandals	รองเท้าแตะ	rorng tháo dtàe
cobbler (shoe repairer)	คนซ่อมรองเท้า	khon sôrm rorng tháo
heel	ส้นรองเท้า	sôn rorng tháo
pair (of shoes)	คู่	khôo
shoestring	เชือกรองเท้า	chêuak rorng tháo
to lace (vt)	ผูกเชือกรองเท้า	phòok chêuak rorng tháo
shoehorn	ที่ซอนรองเท้า	thêe chón rorng tháo
shoe polish	ยาขัดรองเท้า	yaa khàt rorng tháo

37. Personal accessories

gloves	ถุงมือ	thǔng meu
mittens	ถุงมือ	thǔng meu
scarf (muffler)	ผ้าพันคอ	phâa phan khor
glasses (eyeglasses)	แว่นตา	wâen dtaa
frame (eyeglass ~)	กรอบแว่น	gròrp wâen
umbrella	ร่ม	rôm
walking stick	ไม้เท้า	máai tháo
hairbrush	แปรงหวีผม	bpraeng wěe phǒm
fan	พัด	phát
tie (necktie)	เนคไท	nâyk-thai
bow tie	โบว์หูกระต่าย	boh hǒo grà-dtàai
suspenders	สายเอี๊ยม	sǎai íam
handkerchief	ผ้าเช็ดหน้า	phâa chét-nâa
comb	หวี	wěe
barrette	ที่หนีบผม	têe nèep phǒm
hairpin	กิ๊บ	gíp
buckle	หัวเข็มขัด	hǔa khěm khàt
belt	เข็มขัด	khěm khàt
shoulder strap	สายกระเป๋า	sǎai grà-bpǎo
bag (handbag)	กระเป๋า	grà-bpǎo
purse	กระเป๋าถือ	grà-bpǎo thěu
backpack	กระเป๋าสะพายหลัง	grà-bpǎo sà-phaai lǎng

38. Clothing. Miscellaneous

fashion	แฟชั่น	fae-chân
in vogue (adj)	คานิยม	khâa ní-yom
fashion designer	นักออกแบบแฟชั่น	nák òrk bàep fae-chân
collar	คอปกเสื้อ	khor bpòk sêua
pocket	กระเป๋า	grà-bpǎo
pocket (as adj)	กระเป๋า	grà-bpǎo
sleeve	แขนเสื้อ	khǎen sêua
hanging loop	ที่แขวนเสื้อ	thêe khwǎen sêua
fly (on trousers)	ซิปกางเกง	síp gaang-gayng
zipper (fastener)	ซิป	síp
fastener	ซิป	síp
button	กระดุม	grà dum
buttonhole	รูกระดุม	roo grà dum
to come off (ab. button)	หลุดออก	lùt òrk
to sew (vi, vt)	เย็บ	yép
to embroider (vi, vt)	ปัก	bpàk
embroidery	ลายปัก	laai bpàk
sewing needle	เข็มเย็บผ้า	khěm yép phâa
thread	เส้นด้าย	sây-dâai
seam	รอยเย็บ	roi yép
to get dirty (vi)	สกปรก	sòk-gà-bpròk
stain (mark, spot)	รอยเปื้อน	roi bpêuan
to crease, crumple (vi)	พับเป็นรอยยน	pháp bpen roi yôn
to tear, to rip (vt)	ฉีก	chèek
clothes moth	แมลงกินผ้า	má-laeng gin phâa

39. Personal care. Cosmetics

toothpaste	ยาสีฟัน	yaa sěe fan
toothbrush	แปรงสีฟัน	bpraeng sěe fan
to brush one's teeth	แปรงฟัน	bpraeng fan
razor	มีดโกน	mêet gohn
shaving cream	ครีมโกนหนวด	khreem gohn nùat
to shave (vi)	โกน	gohn
soap	สบู่	sà-bòo
shampoo	แชมพู	chaem-phoo
scissors	กรรไกร	gan-grai
nail file	ตะไบเล็บ	dtà-bai lép
nail clippers	กรรไกรตัดเล็บ	gan-grai dtàt lép
tweezers	แหนบ	nàep

cosmetics	เครื่องสำอาง	khrêuang sǎm-aang
face mask	มาสกหุน้า	mâak nâa
manicure	การแต่งเล็บ	gaan dtàeng lép
to have a manicure	แต่งเล็บ	dtàeng lép
pedicure	การแต่งเล็บเท้า	gaan dtàeng lép táo

make-up bag	กระเป๋าเครื่อง สำอาง	grà-bpǎo khrêuang sǎm-aang
face powder	แป้งฝุ่น	bpâeng-fùn
powder compact	ตลับแป้ง	dtà-làp bpâeng
blusher	แป้งทาแก้ม	bpâeng thaa gâem

perfume (bottled)	น้ำหอม	nám hǒrm
toilet water (lotion)	น้ำหอมออนๆ	náam hǒrm òn òn
lotion	โลชั่น	loh-chân
cologne	โคโลญจ์	khoh-lohn

eyeshadow	อายแชโดว์	aai-chae-doh
eyeliner	อายไลเนอร์	aai lai-ner
mascara	มาสคารา	mâat-khaa-râa

lipstick	ลิปสติก	líp-sà-dtìk
nail polish, enamel	น้ำยาทาเล็บ	nám yaa-thaa lép
hair spray	สเปรย์ฉีดผม	sà-bpray chèet phǒm
deodorant	ยาดับกลิ่น	yaa dàp glìn

cream	ครีม	khreem
face cream	ครีมทาหน้า	khreem thaa nâa
hand cream	ครีมทามือ	khreem thaa meu
anti-wrinkle cream	ครีมลดริ้วรอย	khreem lót ríw roi
day cream	ครีมกลางวัน	khreem klaang wan
night cream	ครีมกลางคืน	khreem klaang kheun
day (as adj)	กลางวัน	glaang wan
night (as adj)	กลางคืน	glaang kheun

tampon	ผ้าอนามัยแบบสอด	phâa a-naa-mai bàep sòrt
toilet paper (toilet roll)	กระดาษชำระ	grà-dàat cham-rá
hair dryer	เครื่องเป่าผม	khrêuang bpào phǒm

40. Watches. Clocks

watch (wristwatch)	นาฬิกา	naa-lí-gaa
dial	หน้าปัด	nâa bpàt
hand (of clock, watch)	เข็ม	khěm
metal watch band	สายนาฬิกาข้อมือ	sǎai naa-lí-gaa khôr meu
watch strap	สายรัดข้อมือ	sǎai rát khôr meu

battery	แบตเตอรี่	bàet-dter-rêe
to be dead (battery)	หมด	mòt
to change a battery	เปลี่ยนแบตเตอรี่	bplìan bàet-dter-rêe

to run fast	เดินเร็วเกินไป	dern reo gern bpai
to run slow	เดินช้า	dern cháa
wall clock	นาฬิกา	naa-lí-gaa
	แขวนผนัง	khwǎen phà-nǎng
hourglass	นาฬิกาทราย	naa-lí-gaa saai
sundial	นาฬิกาแดด	naa-lí-gaa dàet
alarm clock	นาฬิกาปลุก	naa-lí-gaa bplùk
watchmaker	ช่างซ่อมนาฬิกา	châang sôrm naa-lí-gaa
to repair (vt)	ซ่อม	sôrm

EVERYDAY EXPERIENCE

41. Money

money	เงิน	ngern
currency exchange	การแลกเปลี่ยน สกุลเงิน	gaan lâek bplìan sà-gun ngern
exchange rate	อัตราแลกเปลี่ยน สกุลเงิน	àt-dtraa lâek bplìan sà-gun ngern
ATM	เอทีเอ็ม	ay-thee-em
coin	เหรียญ	rĭan
dollar	ดอลลาร์	dorn-lâa
euro	ยูโร	yoo-roh
lira	ลีราอิตาลี	lee-raa ì-dtaa-lee
Deutschmark	มาร์ค	mâak
franc	ฟรังค์	frang
pound sterling	ปอนด์สเตอร์ลิง	bporn sà-dtêr-ling
yen	เยน	yayn
debt	หนี้	nêe
debtor	ลูกหนี้	lôok nêe
to lend (money)	ให้ยืม	hâi yeum
to borrow (vi, vt)	ขอยืม	khŏr yeum
bank	ธนาคาร	thá-naa-khaan
account	บัญชี	ban-chee
to deposit (vt)	ฝาก	fàak
to deposit into the account	ฝากเงินเข้าบัญชี	fàak ngern khâo ban-chee
to withdraw (vt)	ถอน	thŏrn
credit card	บัตรเครดิต	bàt khray-dìt
cash	เงินสด	ngern sòt
check	เช็ค	chék
to write a check	เขียนเช็ค	khĭan chék
checkbook	สมุดเช็ค	sà-mùt chék
wallet	กระเป๋าเงิน	grà-bpăo ngern
change purse	กระเป๋าสตางค์	grà-bpăo sà-dtaang
safe	ตู้เซฟ	dtôo sâyf
heir	ทายาท	thaa-yâat
inheritance	มรดก	mor-rá-dòrk
fortune (wealth)	เงินจำนวนมาก	ngern jam-nuan mâak
lease	สัญญาเช่า	săn-yaa châo

rent (money)	ค่าเช่า	kâa châo
to rent (sth from sb)	เช่า	châo
price	ราคา	raa-khaa
cost	ราคา	raa-khaa
sum	จำนวนเงินรวม	jam-nuan ngern ruam
to spend (vt)	จ่าย	jàai
expenses	ค่าจ่าย	khâa jàai
to economize (vi, vt)	ประหยัด	bprà-yàt
economical	ประหยัด	bprà-yàt
to pay (vi, vt)	จ่าย	jàai
payment	การจ่ายเงิน	gaan jàai ngern
change (give the ~)	เงินทอน	ngern thorn
tax	ภาษี	phaa-sĕe
fine	ค่าปรับ	khâa bpràp
to fine (vt)	ปรับ	bpràp

42. Post. Postal service

post office	โรงไปรษณีย์	rohng bprai-sà-nee
mail (letters, etc.)	จดหมาย	jòt măai
mailman	บุรุษไปรษณีย์	bù-rùt bprai-sà-nee
opening hours	เวลาทำการ	way-laa tham gaan
letter	จดหมาย	jòt măai
registered letter	จดหมายลงทะเบียน	jòt măai long thá-bian
postcard	ไปรษณียบัตร	bprai-sà-nee-yá-bàt
telegram	โทรเลข	thoh-rá-lâyk
package (parcel)	พัสดุ	phát-sà-dù
money transfer	การโอนเงิน	gaan ohn ngern
to receive (vt)	รับ	ráp
to send (vt)	ฝาก	fàak
sending	การฝาก	gaan fàak
address	ที่อยู่	thêe yòo
ZIP code	รหัสไปรษณีย์	rá-hàt bprai-sà-nee
sender	ผู้ฝาก	phôo fàak
receiver	ผู้รับ	phôo ráp
name (first name)	ชื่อ	chêu
surname (last name)	นามสกุล	naam sà-gun
postage rate	อัตราค่าส่งไปรษณีย์	àt-dtraa khâa sòng bprai-sà-nee
standard (adj)	มาตรฐาน	mâat-dtrà-thăan
economical (adj)	ประหยัด	bprà-yàt

weight	น้ำหนัก	nám nàk
to weigh (~ letters)	มีน้ำหนัก	mee nám nàk
envelope	ซอง	sorng
postage stamp	แสตมป์ไปรษณีย์	sà-dtaem bprai-sà-nee
to stamp an envelope	แสตมป์ตรา ประทับบนซอง	sà-dtaem dtraa bprà-tháp bon song

43. Banking

bank	ธนาคาร	thá-naa-khaan
branch (of bank, etc.)	สาขา	săa-khăa
bank clerk, consultant	พนักงาน ธนาคาร	phá-nák ngaan thá-naa-khaan
manager (director)	ผู้จัดการ	phôo jàt gaan
bank account	บัญชีธนาคาร	ban-chee thá-naa-kaan
account number	หมายเลขบัญชี	măai lâyk ban-chee
checking account	กระแสรายวัน	grà-săe raai wan
savings account	บัญชีออมทรัพย์	ban-chee orm sáp
to open an account	เปิดบัญชี	bpèrt ban-chee
to close the account	ปิดบัญชี	bpìt ban-chee
to deposit into the account	ฝากเงินเข้าบัญชี	fàak ngern khâo ban-chee
to withdraw (vt)	ถอน	thŏrn
deposit	การฝาก	gaan fàak
to make a deposit	ฝาก	fàak
wire transfer	การโอนเงิน	gaan ohn ngern
to wire, to transfer	โอนเงิน	ohn ngern
sum	จำนวนเงินรวม	jam-nuan ngern ruam
How much?	เท่าไหร่?	thâo rài
signature	ลายมือชื่อ	laai meu chêu
to sign (vt)	ลงนาม	long naam
credit card	บัตรเครดิต	bàt khray-dìt
code (PIN code)	รหัส	rá-hàt
credit card number	หมายเลขบัตรเครดิต	măai lâyk bàt khray-dìt
ATM	เอทีเอ็ม	ay-thee-em
check	เช็ค	chék
to write a check	เขียนเช็ค	khĭan chék
checkbook	สมุดเช็ค	sà-mùt chék
loan (bank ~)	เงินกู้	ngern gôo
to apply for a loan	ขอสินเชื่อ	khŏr sĭn chêua
to get a loan	กู้เงิน	gôo ngern
to give a loan	ให้กู้เงิน	hâi gôo ngern
guarantee	การรับประกัน	gaan ráp bprà-gan

44. Telephone. Phone conversation

telephone	โทรศัพท์	thoh-rá-sàp
cell phone	มือถือ	meu thĕu
answering machine	เครื่องพูดตอบ	khrêuang phôot dtòp
to call (by phone)	โทรศัพท์	thoh-rá-sàp
phone call	การโทรศัพท์	gaan thoh-rá-sàp
to dial a number	หมุนหมายเลขโทรศัพท์	mŭn măai lâyk thoh-rá-sàp
Hello!	สวัสดี!	sà-wàt-dee
to ask (vt)	ถาม	thăam
to answer (vi, vt)	รับสาย	ráp săai
to hear (vt)	ได้ยิน	dâai yin
well (adv)	ดี	dee
not well (adv)	ไม่ดี	mâi dee
noises (interference)	เสียงรบกวน	sĭang róp guan
receiver	ตัวรับสัญญาณ	dtua ráp săn-yaan
to pick up (~ the phone)	รับสาย	ráp săai
to hang up (~ the phone)	วางสาย	waang săai
busy (engaged)	ไม่ว่าง	mâi wâang
to ring (ab. phone)	ดัง	dang
telephone book	สมุดโทรศัพท์	sà-mùt thoh-rá-sàp
local (adj)	ในประเทศ	nai bprà-thâyt
local call	โทรในประเทศ	thoh nai bprà-thâyt
long distance (~ call)	ระยะไกล	rá-yá glai
long-distance call	โทรระยะไกล	thoh-rá-yá glai
international (adj)	ต่างประเทศ	dtàang bprà-thâyt
international call	โทรต่างประเทศ	thoh dtàang bprà-thâyt

45. Cell phone

cell phone	มือถือ	meu thĕu
display	หน้าจอ	nâa jor
button	ปุ่ม	bpùm
SIM card	ซิมการ์ด	sím gàat
battery	แบตเตอรี่	bàet-dter-rêe
to be dead (battery)	หมด	mòt
charger	ที่ชาร์จ	thêe châat
menu	เมนู	may-noo
settings	การตั้งค่า	gaan dtâng khâa
tune (melody)	เสียงเพลง	sĭang phlayng
to select (vt)	เลือก	lêuak

calculator	เครื่องคิดเลข	khrêuang khít lâyk
voice mail	ขอความเสียง	khôr khwaam sĭang
alarm clock	นาฬิกาปลุก	naa-lí-gaa bplùk
contacts	รายชื่อผู้ติดต่อ	raai chêu phôo dtìt dtòr

| SMS (text message) | ŞMS | es-e-mes |
| subscriber | ผู้สมัครรับ
บริการ | phôo sà-màk ráp
bor-rí-gaan |

46. Stationery

| ballpoint pen | ปากกาลูกลื่น | bpàak gaa lôok lêun |
| fountain pen | ปากกาหมึกซึม | bpàak gaa mèuk seum |

pencil	ดินสอ	din-sŏr
highlighter	ปากกาเน้น	bpàak gaa náyn
felt-tip pen	ปากกาเมจิด	bpàak gaa may jìk

| notepad | สมุดจด | sà-mùt jòt |
| agenda (diary) | สมุดบันทึกรายวัน | sà-mùt ban-théuk raai wan |

ruler	ไม้บรรทัด	máai ban-thát
calculator	เครื่องคิดเลข	khrêuang khít lâyk
eraser	ยางลบ	yaang lóp
thumbtack	เป๊ก	bpáyk
paper clip	ลวดหนีบกระดาษ	lûat nèep grà-dàat

glue	กาว	gaao
stapler	ที่เย็บกระดาษ	thêe yép grà-dàat
hole punch	ที่เจาะรูกระดาษ	thêe jòr roo grà-dàat
pencil sharpener	ที่เหลาดินสอ	thêe lăo din-sŏr

47. Foreign languages

language	ภาษา	phaa-săa
foreign (adj)	ต่างชาติ	dtàang châat
foreign language	ภาษาต่างชาติ	phaa-săa dtàang châat
to study (vt)	เรียน	rian
to learn (language, etc.)	เรียน	rian

to read (vi, vt)	อ่าน	àan
to speak (vi, vt)	พูด	phôot
to understand (vt)	เข้าใจ	khâo jai
to write (vt)	เขียน	khĭan

fast (adv)	รวดเร็ว	rûat reo
slowly (adv)	อย่างช้า	yàang cháa
fluently (adv)	อย่างคล่อง	yàang khlôrng

rules	กฎ	gòt
grammar	ไวยากรณ์	wai-yaa-gon
vocabulary	คำศัพท์	kham sàp
phonetics	การออกเสียง	gaan òrk sĭang
textbook	หนังสือเรียน	năng-sĕu rian
dictionary	พจนานุกรม	phót-jà-naa-nú-grom
teach-yourself book	หนังสือแบบเรียน ด้วยตนเอง	năng-sĕu bàep rian dûay dton ayng
phrasebook	เฟรสบุก	frayt bùk
cassette, tape	เทปคาสเซ็ตต์	thâyp khaas-sét
videotape	วิดีโอ	wí-dee-oh
CD, compact disc	CD	see-dee
DVD	DVD	dee-wee-dee
alphabet	ตัวอักษร	dtua àk-sŏn
to spell (vt)	สะกด	sà-gòt
pronunciation	การออกเสียง	gaan òrk sĭang
accent	สำเนียง	săm-niang
with an accent	มีสำเนียง	mee săm-niang
without an accent	ไม่มีสำเนียง	mâi mee săm-niang
word	คำ	kham
meaning	ความหมาย	khwaam măai
course (e.g., a French ~)	หลักสูตร	làk sòot
to sign up	สมัคร	sà-màk
teacher	อาจารย์	aa-jaan
translation (process)	การแปล	gaan bplae
translation (text, etc.)	คำแปล	kham bplae
translator	นักแปล	nák bplae
interpreter	ลาม	lâam
polyglot	ผู้รู้หลายภาษา	phôo róo lăai paa-săa
memory	ความทรงจำ	khwaam song jam

MEALS. RESTAURANT

48. Table setting

spoon	ช้อน	chórn
knife	มีด	mêet
fork	ส้อม	sôrm
cup (e.g., coffee ~)	แก้ว	gâew
plate (dinner ~)	จาน	jaan
saucer	จานรอง	jaan rorng
napkin (on table)	ผ้าเช็ดปาก	phâa chét bpàak
toothpick	ไม้จิ้มฟัน	máai jîm fan

49. Restaurant

restaurant	ร้านอาหาร	ráan aa-hăan
coffee house	ร้านกาแฟ	ráan gaa-fae
pub, bar	ร้านเหล้า	ráan lâo
tearoom	ร้านน้ำชา	ráan nám chaa
waiter	คนเสิร์ฟชาย	khon sèrf chaai
waitress	คนเสิร์ฟหญิง	khon sèrf yĭng
bartender	บาร์เทนเดอร์	baa-thayn-dêr
menu	เมนู	may-noo
wine list	รายการไวน์	raai gaan wai
to book a table	จองโต๊ะ	jorng dtó
course, dish	มื้ออาหาร	méu aa-hăan
to order (meal)	สั่ง	sàng
to make an order	สั่งอาหาร	sàng aa-hăan
aperitif	เครื่องดื่มเหล้า กอนอาหาร	khrêuang dèum lâo gòrn aa-hăan
appetizer	ของกินเล่น	khŏrng gin lâyn
dessert	ของหวาน	khŏrng wăan
check	คิดเงิน	khít ngern
to pay the check	จ่ายค่าอาหาร	jàai khâa aa hăan
to give change	ให้เงินทอน	hâi ngern thorn
tip	เงินทิป	ngern thíp

50. Meals

| food | อาหาร | aa-hăan |
| to eat (vi, vt) | กิน | gin |

breakfast	อาหารเช้า	aa-hăan cháo
to have breakfast	ทานอาหารเช้า	thaan aa-hăan cháo
lunch	ขาวเที่ยง	khâao thîang
to have lunch	ทานอาหารเที่ยง	thaan aa-hăan thîang
dinner	อาหารเย็น	aa-hăan yen
to have dinner	ทานอาหารเย็น	thaan aa-hăan yen

| appetite | ความอยากอาหาร | kwaam yàak aa hăan |
| Enjoy your meal! | กินให้อรอย! | gin hâi a-ròi |

to open (~ a bottle)	เปิด	bpèrt
to spill (liquid)	ทำหก	tham hòk
to spill out (vi)	ทำหกออกมา	tham hòk òrk maa

to boil (vi)	ต้ม	dtôm
to boil (vt)	ต้ม	dtôm
boiled (~ water)	ต้ม	dtôm
to chill, cool down (vt)	แชเย็น	châe yen
to chill (vi)	แชเย็น	châe yen

| taste, flavor | รสชาติ | rót châat |
| aftertaste | รส | rót |

to slim down (lose weight)	ลดน้ำหนัก	lót nám nàk
diet	อาหารพิเศษ	aa-hăan phí-sàyt
vitamin	วิตามิน	wí-dtaa-min
calorie	แคลอรี่	khae-lor-rêe
vegetarian (n)	คนกินเจ	khon gin jay
vegetarian (adj)	มังสวิรัติ	mang-sà-wí-rát

fats (nutrient)	ไขมัน	khăi man
proteins	โปรตีน	bproh-dteen
carbohydrates	คาร์โบไฮเดรต	kaa-boh-hai-dràyt

slice (of lemon, ham)	แผ่น	phàen
piece (of cake, pie)	ชิ้น	chín
crumb (of bread, cake, etc.)	เศษ	sàyt

51. Cooked dishes

course, dish	มื้ออาหาร	méu aa-hăan
cuisine	อาหาร	aa-hăan
recipe	ตำราอาหาร	dtam-raa aa-hăan

portion	ส่วน	sùan
salad	สลัด	sà-làt
soup	ซุป	súp
clear soup (broth)	ซุปน้ำใส	súp nám-săi
sandwich (bread)	แชนด์วิช	saen-wít
fried eggs	ไข่ทอด	khài thôrt
hamburger (beefburger)	แฮมเบอร์เกอร์	haem-ber-gêr
beefsteak	สเต็กเนื้อ	sà-dtèk néua
side dish	เครื่องเคียง	khrêuang khiang
spaghetti	สปาเก็ตตี้	sà-bpaa-gèt-dtêe
mashed potatoes	มันฝรั่งบด	man fà-ràng bòt
pizza	พิซซ่า	phít-sâa
porridge (oatmeal, etc.)	ข้าวต้ม	khâao-dtôm
omelet	ไข่เจียว	khài jieow
boiled (e.g., ~ beef)	ต้ม	dtôm
smoked (adj)	รมควัน	rom khwan
fried (adj)	ทอด	thôrt
dried (adj)	ตากแห้ง	dtàak hâeng
frozen (adj)	แช่แข็ง	châe khăeng
pickled (adj)	ดอง	dorng
sweet (sugary)	หวาน	wăan
salty (adj)	เค็ม	khem
cold (adj)	เย็น	yen
hot (adj)	ร้อน	rórn
bitter (adj)	ขม	khŏm
tasty (adj)	อร่อย	à-ròi
to cook in boiling water	ต้ม	dtôm
to cook (dinner)	ทำอาหาร	tham aa-hăan
to fry (vt)	ทอด	thôrt
to heat up (food)	อุ่น	ùn
to salt (vt)	ใส่เกลือ	sài gleua
to pepper (vt)	ใส่พริกไทย	sài phrík thai
to grate (vt)	ขูด	khòot
peel (n)	เปลือก	bplèuak
to peel (vt)	ปอกเปลือก	bpòrk bplêuak

52. Food

meat	เนื้อ	néua
chicken	ไก่	gài
Rock Cornish hen (poussin)	เนื้อลูกไก่	néua lôok gài
duck	เป็ด	bpèt

goose	ห่าน	hàan
game	สัตว์ที่ล่า	sàt thêe lâa
turkey	ไก่งวง	gài nguang
pork	เนื้อหมู	néua mǒo
veal	เนื้อลูกวัว	néua lôok wua
lamb	เนื้อแกะ	néua gàe
beef	เนื้อวัว	néua wua
rabbit	เนื้อกระต่าย	néua grà-dtàai
sausage (bologna, etc.)	ไส้กรอก	sâi gròrk
vienna sausage (frankfurter)	ไส้กรอกเวียนนา	sâi gròrk wian-naa
bacon	หมูเบคอน	mǒo bay-khorn
ham	แฮม	haem
gammon	แฮมแกมมอน	haem gaem-morn
pâté	ปาเต	bpaa dtay
liver	ตับ	dtàp
hamburger (ground beef)	เนื้อสับ	néua sàp
tongue	ลิ้น	lín
egg	ไข่	khài
eggs	ไข่	khài
egg white	ไข่ขาว	khài khǎao
egg yolk	ไข่แดง	khài daeng
fish	ปลา	bplaa
seafood	อาหารทะเล	aa hǎan thá-lay
crustaceans	สัตว์พวกกุ้งกั้งปู	sàt phûak gûng gâng bpoo
caviar	ไข่ปลา	khài-bplaa
crab	ปู	bpoo
shrimp	กุ้ง	gûng
oyster	หอยนางรม	hǒi naang rom
spiny lobster	กุ้งมังกร	gûng mang-gon
octopus	ปลาหมึก	bplaa mèuk
squid	ปลาหมึกกล้วย	bplaa mèuk-glûay
sturgeon	ปลาสเตอร์เจียน	bpláa sà-dtêr jian
salmon	ปลาแซลมอน	bplaa saen-morn
halibut	ปลาตาเดียว	bplaa dtaa-dieow
cod	ปลาค็อด	bplaa khót
mackerel	ปลาแม็คเคอเร็ล	bplaa máek-kay-a-rěn
tuna	ปลาทูน่า	bplaa thoo-nâa
eel	ปลาไหล	bplaa lǎi
trout	ปลาเทราท์	bplaa thrau
sardine	ปลาซาร์ดีน	bplaa saa-deen
pike	ปลาไพค์	bplaa phai
herring	ปลาเฮอร์ริ่ง	bplaa her-ring

bread	ขนมปัง	khà-nòm bpang
cheese	เนยแข็ง	noie khǎeng
sugar	น้ำตาล	nám dtaan
salt	เกลือ	gleua
rice	ข้าว	khâao
pasta (macaroni)	พาสต้า	phâat-dtâa
noodles	กวยเตี๋ยว	gǔay-dtǐeow
butter	เนย	noie
vegetable oil	น้ำมันพืช	nám man phêut
sunflower oil	น้ำมันดอก	nám man dòrk
	ทานตะวัน	thaan dtà-wan
margarine	เนยเทียม	noie thiam
olives	มะกอก	má-gòrk
olive oil	น้ำมันมะกอก	nám man má-gòrk
milk	นม	nom
condensed milk	นมขัน	nom khôn
yogurt	โยเกิร์ต	yoh-gèrt
sour cream	ซาวรครีม	saao khreem
cream (of milk)	ครีม	khreem
mayonnaise	มาย็องเนส	maa-yorng-nâyt
buttercream	สวนผสมของเนย	sùan phà-sǒm khǒrng
	และน้ำตาล	noie láe nám dtaan
groats (barley ~, etc.)	เมล็ดธัญพืช	má-lét than-yá-phêut
flour	แป้ง	bpâeng
canned food	อาหารกระป๋อง	aa-hǎan grà-bpǒrng
cornflakes	คอร์นเฟลค	khorn-flâyk
honey	น้ำผึ้ง	nám phêung
jam	แยม	yaem
chewing gum	หมากฝรั่ง	màak fà-ràng

53. Drinks

water	น้ำ	nám
drinking water	น้ำดื่ม	nám dèum
mineral water	น้ำแร่	nám râe
still (adj)	ไม่มีฟอง	mâi mee forng
carbonated (adj)	น้ำอัดลม	nám àt lom
sparkling (adj)	มีฟอง	mee forng
ice	น้ำแข็ง	nám khǎeng
with ice	ใส่น้ำแข็ง	sài nám khǎeng
non-alcoholic (adj)	ไม่มีแอลกอฮอล์	mâi mee aen-gor-hor
soft drink	เครื่องดื่มที่	krêuang dèum têe
	ไม่มีแอลกอฮอล์	mâi mee aen-gor-hor

refreshing drink	เครื่องดื่มให้ความสดชื่น	khrêuang dèum hâi khwaam sòt chêun
lemonade	น้ำเลมอนเนด	nám lay-morn-nâyt
liquors	เหล้า	lǎu
wine	ไวน์	wai
white wine	ไวน์ขาว	wai khǎao
red wine	ไวน์แดง	wai daeng
liqueur	สุรา	sù-raa
champagne	แชมเปญ	chaem-bpayn
vermouth	เหล้าองุ่นขาวซึ่งมีกลิ่นหอม	lâo a-ngùn khǎao sêung mee glìn hǒrm
whiskey	เหล้าวิสกี้	lǎu wít-sa -gêe
vodka	เหล้าวอดก้า	lǎu wórt-gâa
gin	เหล้ายิน	lǎu yin
cognac	เหล้าคอนยัก	lǎu khorn yák
rum	เหล้ารัม	lǎu ram
coffee	กาแฟ	gaa-fae
black coffee	กาแฟดำ	gaa-fae dam
coffee with milk	กาแฟใส่นม	gaa-fae sài nom
cappuccino	กาแฟคาปูชิโน	gaa-fae khaa bpoo chí noh
instant coffee	กาแฟสำเร็จรูป	gaa-fae sǎm-rèt rôop
milk	นม	nom
cocktail	ค็อกเทล	khók-tayn
milkshake	มิลค์เชค	min-châyk
juice	น้ำผลไม้	nám phǒn-lá-máai
tomato juice	น้ำมะเขือเทศ	nám má-khěua thâyt
orange juice	น้ำส้ม	nám sôm
freshly squeezed juice	น้ำผลไม้คั้นสด	nám phǒn-lá-máai khán sòt
beer	เบียร์	bia
light beer	เบียร์ไลท์	bia lai
dark beer	เบียร์ดารค	bia dàak
tea	ชา	chaa
black tea	ชาดำ	chaa dam
green tea	ชาเขียว	chaa khǐeow

54. Vegetables

vegetables	ผัก	phàk
greens	ผักใบเขียว	phàk bai khǐeow
tomato	มะเขือเทศ	má-khěua thâyt
cucumber	แตงกวา	dtaeng-gwaa

carrot	แครอท	khae-rót
potato	มันฝรั่ง	man fà-ràng
onion	หัวหอม	hǔa hǒrm
garlic	กระเทียม	grà-thiam

cabbage	กะหล่ำปลี	gà-làm bplee
cauliflower	ดอกกะหล่ำ	dòrk gà-làm
Brussels sprouts	กะหล่ำดาว	gà-làm-daao
broccoli	บร็อคโคลี่	bròrk-khoh-lêe

beet	บีทรูท	bee-trôot
eggplant	มะเขือยาว	má-khěua-yaao
zucchini	แตงซูคินี	dtaeng soo-khí-nee
pumpkin	ฟักทอง	fák-thorng
turnip	หัวผักกาด	hǔa-phàk-gàat

parsley	ผักชีฝรั่ง	phàk chee fà-ràng
dill	ผักชีลาว	phàk-chee-laao
lettuce	ผักกาดหอม	phàk gàat hǒrm
celery	คื่นช่าย	khêun-châai
asparagus	หน่อไม้ฝรั่ง	nòr máai fà-ràng
spinach	ผักขม	phàk khǒm

pea	ถั่วลันเตา	thùa-lan-dtao
beans	ถั่ว	thùa
corn (maize)	ข้าวโพด	khâao-phôht
kidney bean	ถั่วรูปไต	thùa rôop dtai

bell pepper	พริกหยวก	phrík-yùak
radish	หัวไชเท้า	hǔa chai tháo
artichoke	อาร์ติโชค	aa dtì chôhk

55. Fruits. Nuts

fruit	ผลไม้	phǒn-lá-máai
apple	แอปเปิ้ล	àep-bpêrn
pear	แพร	phae
lemon	มะนาว	má-naao
orange	ส้ม	sôm
strawberry (garden ~)	สตรอว์เบอร์รี่	sà-dtror-ber-rêe

mandarin	ส้มแมนดาริน	sôm maen daa rin
plum	พลัม	phlam
peach	ลูกท้อ	lôok thór
apricot	แอปริคอท	ae-bprì-khôrt
raspberry	ราสเบอร์รี่	râat-ber-rêe
pineapple	สับปะรด	sàp-bpà-rót

| banana | กล้วย | glûay |
| watermelon | แตงโม | dtaeng moh |

grape	องุ่น	a-ngùn
sour cherry	เชอร์รี่	cher-rêe
sweet cherry	เชอร์รี่ป่า	cher-rêe bpàa
melon	เมลอน	may-lorn
grapefruit	ส้มโอ	sôm oh
avocado	อะโวคาโด	a-who-khaa-doh
papaya	มะละกอ	má-lá-gor
mango	มะม่วง	má-mûang
pomegranate	ทับทิม	tháp-thim
redcurrant	เรดเคอร์แรนท์	râyt-khêr-raen
blackcurrant	แบล็คเคอูรแรนท์	blàek khêr-raen
gooseberry	กูสเบอร์รี่	gòot-ber-rêe
bilberry	บิลเบอร์รี่	bil-ber-rêe
blackberry	แบล็คเบอร์รี่	blàek ber-rêe
raisin	ลูกเกด	lôok gàyt
fig	มะเดื่อฝรั่ง	má dèua fà-ràng
date	ลูกอินทผลัม	lôok in-thá-plăm
peanut	ถั่วลิสง	thùa-lí-sŏng
almond	อัลมอนด์	an-morn
walnut	วอลนัต	wor-lá-nát
hazelnut	เฮเซลนัท	hay sayn nát
coconut	มะพร้าว	má-phráao
pistachios	ถั่วพิสตาชิโอ	thùa phít dtaa chí oh

56. Bread. Candy

bakers' confectionery (pastry)	ขนม	khà-nŏm
bread	ขนมปัง	khà-nŏm bpang
cookies	คุกกี้	khúk-gêe
chocolate (n)	ช็อกโกแลต	chók-goh-láet
chocolate (as adj)	ช็อกโกแลต	chók-goh-láet
candy (wrapped)	ลูกกวาด	lôok gwàat
cake (e.g., cupcake)	ขนมเค้ก	khà-nŏm kháyk
cake (e.g., birthday ~)	ขนมเค้ก	khà-nŏm kháyk
pie (e.g., apple ~)	ขนมพาย	khà-nŏm phaai
filling (for cake, pie)	ไส้ในขนม	sâi nai khà-nŏm
jam (whole fruit jam)	แยม	yaem
marmalade	แยมผิวส้ม	yaem phĭw sôm
wafers	วาฟเฟิล	waaf-fern
ice-cream	ไอศกรีม	ai-sà-greem
pudding	พุดดิ้ง	phút-dîng

57. Spices

salt	เกลือ	gleua
salty (adj)	เค็ม	khem
to salt (vt)	ใส่เกลือ	sài gleua
black pepper	พริกไทย	phrík thai
red pepper (milled ~)	พริกแดง	phrík daeng
mustard	มัสตารด	mát-dtàat
horseradish	ฮอสแรดิช	hórt rae dìt
condiment	เครื่องปรุงรส	khrêuang bprung rót
spice	เครื่องเทศ	khrêuang thâyt
sauce	ซอส	sós
vinegar	น้ำสมสายชู	nám sôm sǎai choo
anise	เทียนสัตตบุษย์	thian-sàt-dtà-bùt
basil	ใบโหระพา	bai hǒh rá phaa
cloves	กานพลู	gaan-phloo
ginger	ขิง	khǐng
coriander	ผักชีลา	pàk-chee-laa
cinnamon	อบเชย	òp-choie
sesame	งา	ngaa
bay leaf	ใบกระวาน	bai grà-waan
paprika	พริกป่น	phrík bpòn
caraway	เทียนตากบ	thian dtaa gòp
saffron	หญ้าฝรั่น	yâa fà-ràn

PERSONAL INFORMATION. FAMILY

58. Personal information. Forms

name (first name)	ชื่อ	chêu
surname (last name)	นามสกุล	naam sà-gun
date of birth	วันเกิด	wan gèrt
place of birth	สถานที่เกิด	sà-thǎan thêe gèrt
nationality	สัญชาติ	sǎn-châat
place of residence	ที่อยู่อาศัย	thêe yòo aa-sǎi
country	ประเทศ	bprà-thâyt
profession (occupation)	อาชีพ	aa-chêep
gender, sex	เพศ	phâyt
height	ความสูง	khwaam sǒong
weight	น้ำหนัก	nám nàk

59. Family members. Relatives

mother	มารดา	maan-daa
father	บิดา	bì-daa
son	ลูกชาย	lôok chaai
daughter	ลูกสาว	lôok sǎao
younger daughter	ลูกสาวคนเล็ก	lôok sǎao khon lék
younger son	ลูกชายคนเล็ก	lôok chaai khon lék
eldest daughter	ลูกสาวคนโต	lôok sǎao khon dtoh
eldest son	ลูกชายคนโต	lôok chaai khon dtoh
elder brother	พี่ชาย	phêe chaai
younger brother	น้องชาย	nórng chaai
elder sister	พี่สาว	phêe sǎao
younger sister	น้องสาว	nórng sǎao
cousin (masc.)	ลูกพี่ลูกน้อง	lôok phêe lôok nórng
cousin (fem.)	ลูกพี่ลูกน้อง	lôok phêe lôok nórng
mom, mommy	แม่	mâe
dad, daddy	พ่อ	phôr
parents	พ่อแม่	phôr mâe
child	เด็ก, ลูก	dèk, lôok
children	เด็กๆ	dèk dèk
grandmother	ย่า, ยาย	yâa, yaai

grandfather	ปู่, ตา	bpòo, dtaa
grandson	หลานชาย	lăan chaai
granddaughter	หลานสาว	lăan săao
grandchildren	หลานๆ	lăan
uncle	ลุง	lung
aunt	ป้า	bpâa
nephew	หลานชาย	lăan chaai
niece	หลานสาว	lăan săao
mother-in-law (wife's mother)	แมยาย	mâe yaai
father-in-law (husband's father)	พ่อสามี	phôr săa-mee
son-in-law (daughter's husband)	ลูกเขย	lôok khŏie
stepmother	แม่เลี้ยง	mâe líang
stepfather	พอเลี้ยง	phôr líang
infant	ทารก	thaa-rók
baby (infant)	เด็กเล็ก	dèk lék
little boy, kid	เด็ก	dèk
wife	ภรรยา	phan-rá-yaa
husband	สามี	săa-mee
spouse (husband)	สามี	săa-mee
spouse (wife)	ภรรยา	phan-rá-yaa
married (masc.)	แต่งงานแล้ว	dtàeng ngaan láew
married (fem.)	แตงงานแลว	dtàeng ngaan láew
single (unmarried)	เป็นโสด	bpen sòht
bachelor	ชายโสด	chaai sòht
divorced (masc.)	หย่าแล้ว	yàa láew
widow	แมหม้าย	mâe mâai
widower	พอหม้าย	phôr mâai
relative	ญาติ	yâat
close relative	ญาติใกล้ชิด	yâat glâi chít
distant relative	ญาติหางๆ	yâat hàang hàang
relatives	ญาติๆ	yâat
orphan (boy)	เด็กชายกำพร้า	dèk chaai gam phráa
orphan (girl)	เด็กหญิงกำพรา	dèk yĭng gam phráa
guardian (of a minor)	ผูปกครอง	phôo bpòk khrorng
to adopt (a boy)	บุญธรรม	bun tham
to adopt (a girl)	บุญธรรม	bun tham

60. Friends. Coworkers

| friend (masc.) | เพื่อน | phêuan |
| friend (fem.) | เพื่อน | phêuan |

friendship	มิตรภาพ	mít-dtrà-phâap
to be friends	เป็นเพื่อน	bpen phêuan
buddy (masc.)	เพื่อนสนิท	phêuan sà-nìt
buddy (fem.)	เพื่อนสนิท	phêuan sà-nìt
partner	หุ้นส่วน	hûn sùan
chief (boss)	หัวหน้า	hŭa-nâa
superior (n)	ผู้บังคับบัญชา	phôo bang-kháp ban-chaa
owner, proprietor	เจ้าของ	jâo khŏrng
subordinate (n)	ลูกน้อง	lôok nórng
colleague	เพื่อนร่วมงาน	phêuan rûam ngaan
acquaintance (person)	ผู้คุ้นเคย	phôo khún khoie
fellow traveler	เพื่อนร่วมทาง	pêuan rûam thaang
classmate	เพื่อนรุ่น	phêuan rûn
neighbor (masc.)	เพื่อนบ้านผู้ชาย	phêuan bâan pôo chaai
neighbor (fem.)	เพื่อนบ้านผู้หญิง	phêuan bâan phôo yǐng
neighbors	เพื่อนบ้าน	phêuan bâan

HUMAN BODY. MEDICINE

61. Head

head	หัว	hŭa
face	หน้า	nâa
nose	จมูก	jà-mòok
mouth	ปาก	bpàak
eye	ตา	dtaa
eyes	ตา	dtaa
pupil	รูม่านตา	roo mâan dtaa
eyebrow	คิ้ว	khíw
eyelash	ขนตา	khŏn dtaa
eyelid	เปลือกตา	bplèuak dtaa
tongue	ลิ้น	lín
tooth	ฟัน	fan
lips	ริมฝีปาก	rim fĕe bpàak
cheekbones	โหนกแก้ม	nòhk gâem
gum	เหงือก	ngèuak
palate	เพดานปาก	phay-daan bpàak
nostrils	รูจมูก	roo jà-mòok
chin	คาง	khaang
jaw	ขากรรไกร	khăa gan-grai
cheek	แก้ม	gâem
forehead	หน้าผาก	nâa phàak
temple	ขมับ	khà-màp
ear	หู	hŏo
back of the head	หลังศีรษะ	lăng sĕe-sà
neck	คอ	khor
throat	ลำคอ	lam khor
hair	ผม	phŏm
hairstyle	ทรงผม	song phŏm
haircut	ทรงผม	song phŏm
wig	ผมปลอม	phŏm bplorm
mustache	หนวด	nùat
beard	เครา	krao
to have (a beard, etc.)	ลองไว้	lorng wái
braid	ผมเปีย	phŏm bpia
sideburns	จอน	jorn
red-haired (adj)	ผมแดง	phŏm daeng

gray (hair)	ผมหงอก	phǒm ngòrk
bald (adj)	หัวล้าน	hǔa láan
bald patch	หัวล้าน	hǔa láan
ponytail	ผมทรงหางม้า	phǒm song hǎang máa
bangs	ผมม้า	phǒm máa

62. Human body

hand	มือ	meu
arm	แขน	khǎen
finger	นิ้ว	níw
toe	นิ้วเท้า	níw tháo
thumb	นิ้วโป้ง	níw bpôhng
little finger	นิ้วก้อย	níw gôi
nail	เล็บ	lép
fist	กำปั้น	gam bpân
palm	ฝ่ามือ	fàa meu
wrist	ข้อมือ	khôr meu
forearm	แขนช่วงล่าง	khǎen chûang lâang
elbow	ข้อศอก	khôr sòrk
shoulder	ไหล่	lài
leg	ขา	khǎa
foot	เท้า	tháo
knee	หัวเข่า	hǔa khào
calf (part of leg)	น่อง	nôrng
hip	สะโพก	sà-phôhk
heel	ส้นเท้า	sôn tháo
body	ร่างกาย	râang gaai
stomach	ท้อง	thórng
chest	อก	òk
breast	หน้าอก	nâa òk
flank	ข้าง	khâang
back	หลัง	lǎng
lower back	หลังส่วนล่าง	lǎng sùan lâang
waist	เอว	eo
navel (belly button)	สะดือ	sà-deu
buttocks	ก้น	gôn
bottom	ก้น	gôn
beauty mark	ไฝเสน่ห์	fǎi sà-này
birthmark (café au lait spot)	ปาน	bpaan
tattoo	รอยสัก	roi sàk
scar	แผลเป็น	phlǎe bpen

63. Diseases

sickness	โรค	rôhk
to be sick	ป่วย	bpùay
health	สุขภาพ	sùk-khà-phâap

runny nose (coryza)	น้ำมูกไหล	nám môok lǎi
tonsillitis	ตอมทอนซิลอักเสบ	dtòm thorn-sin àk-sàyp
cold (illness)	หวัด	wàt
to catch a cold	เป็นหวัด	bpen wàt

bronchitis	โรคหลอดลมอักเสบ	rôhk lòrt lom àk-sàyp
pneumonia	โรคปอดบวม	rôhk bpòrt-buam
flu, influenza	ไขหวัดใหญ	khâi wàt yài

nearsighted (adj)	สายตาสั้น	sǎai dtaa sân
farsighted (adj)	สายตายาว	sǎai dtaa yaao
strabismus (crossed eyes)	ตาเหล	dtaa lày
cross-eyed (adj)	เป็นตาเหล	bpen dtaa kǎy rěu lày
cataract	ตอกระจก	dtôr grà-jòk
glaucoma	ตอหิน	dtôr hǐn

stroke	โรคหลอดเลือดสมอง	rôhk lòrt lêuat sà-mǒrng
heart attack	อาการหัวใจวาย	aa-gaan hǔa jai waai
myocardial infarction	กลามเนื้อหัวใจตาย	glâam néua hǔa jai dtaai
	เหตุขาดเลือด	hàyt khàat lêuat
paralysis	อัมพาต	am-má-phâat
to paralyze (vt)	ทำให้เป็น	tham hâi bpen
	อัมพาต	am-má-phâat

allergy	ภูมิแพ้	phoom pháe
asthma	โรคหืด	rôhk hèut
diabetes	โรคเบาหวาน	rôhk bao wǎan

toothache	อาการปวดฟัน	aa-gaan bpùat fan
caries	ฟันผุ	fan phù

diarrhea	อาการท้องเสีย	aa-gaan thórng sǐa
constipation	อาการทองผูก	aa-gaan thórng phòok
stomach upset	อาการปวดทอง	aa-gaan bpùat thórng
food poisoning	ภาวะอาหารเป็นพิษ	phaa-wá aa hǎan bpen pít
to get food poisoning	กินอาหารเป็นพิษ	gin aa hǎan bpen phít

arthritis	โรคข้ออักเสบ	rôhk khôr àk-sàyp
rickets	โรคกระดูกออน	rôhk grà-dòok òrn
rheumatism	โรครูมาติก	rôhk roo-maa-dtìk
atherosclerosis	ภาวะหลอดเลือดแข็ง	phaa-wá lòrt lêuat khǎeng
gastritis	โรคกระเพาะอาหาร	rôhk grà-phór aa-hǎan
appendicitis	ไสติ่งอักเสบ	sâi dtìng àk-sàyp
cholecystitis	โรคถุงน้ำดี	rôhk thǔng nám dee
	อักเสบ	àk-sàyp

ulcer	แผลเปื่อย	phlǎe bpèuay
measles	โรคหัด	rôhk hàt
rubella (German measles)	โรคหัดเยอรมัน	rôhk hàt yer-rá-man
jaundice	โรคดีซ่าน	rôhk dee sâan
hepatitis	โรคตับอักเสบ	rôhk dtàp àk-sàyp
schizophrenia	โรคจิตเภท	rôhk jìt-dtà-phâyt
rabies (hydrophobia)	โรคพิษสุนัขบ้า	rôhk phít sù-nák bâa
neurosis	โรคประสาท	rôhk bprà-sàat
concussion	สมองกระทบกระเทือน	sà-mǒrng grà-thóp grà-theuan
cancer	มะเร็ง	má-reng
sclerosis	กฎรแข็งตัวของเนื้อเยื่อรางกาย	gaan kǎeng dtua kǒng néua yêua râang gaai
multiple sclerosis	โรคปลอกประสาทเสื่อมแข็ง	rôhk bplòk bprà-sàat sèuam kǎeng
alcoholism	โรคพิษสุราเรื้อรัง	rôhk phít sù-raa réua rang
alcoholic (n)	คนขี้เหล้า	khon khêe lâo
syphilis	โรคซิฟิลิส	rôhk sí-fí-lít
AIDS	โรคเอดส	rôhk àyt
tumor	เนื้องอก	néua ngôk
malignant (adj)	ราย	ráai
benign (adj)	ไม่ราย	mâi ráai
fever	ไข้	khâi
malaria	ไข้มาลาเรีย	kâi maa-laa-ria
gangrene	เนื้อตายเน่า	néua dtaai nâo
seasickness	ภาวะเมาคลื่น	phaa-wá mao khlêun
epilepsy	โรคลมบาหมู	rôhk lom bâa-mǒo
epidemic	โรคระบาด	rôhk rá-bàat
typhus	โรครากสาดใหญ่	rôhk râak-sàat yài
tuberculosis	วัณโรค	wan-ná-rôhk
cholera	อหิวาตกโรค	a-hì-wâat-gà-rôhk
plague (bubonic ~)	กาฬโรค	gaan-lá-rôhk

64. Symptoms. Treatments. Part 1

symptom	อาการ	aa-gaan
temperature	อุณหภูมิ	un-hà-phoom
high temperature (fever)	อุณหภูมิสูง	un-hà-phoom sǒong
pulse (heartbeat)	ชีพจร	chêep-phá-jon
dizziness (vertigo)	อาการเวียนหัว	aa-gaan wian hǔa
hot (adj)	รอน	rórn
shivering	หนาวสั่น	nǎao sàn
pale (e.g., ~ face)	หน้าเชียว	nâa sieow

cough	การไอ	gaan ai
to cough (vi)	ไอ	ai
to sneeze (vi)	จาม	jaam
faint	การเป็นลม	gaan bpen lom
to faint (vi)	เป็นลม	bpen lom

bruise (hématome)	ฟกช้ำ	fók chám
bump (lump)	บวม	buam
to bang (bump)	ชน	chon
contusion (bruise)	รอยฟกช้ำ	roi fók chám
to get a bruise	ได้รอยช้ำ	dâai roi chám

to limp (vi)	กะโผลกกะเผลก	gà-phlòhk-gà-phlàyk
dislocation	ขอหลุด	khôr lùt
to dislocate (vt)	ทำขอหลุด	tham khôr lùt
fracture	กระดูกหัก	grà-dòok hàk
to have a fracture	หักกระดูก	hàk grà-dòok

cut (e.g., paper ~)	รอยบาด	roi bàat
to cut oneself	ทำบาด	tham bàat
bleeding	การเลือดไหล	gaan lêuat lǎi

| burn (injury) | แผลไฟไหม้ | phlǎe fai mâi |
| to get burned | ได้รับแผลไฟไหม้ | dâai ráp phlǎe fai mâi |

to prick (vt)	ตำ	dtam
to prick oneself	ตำตัวเอง	dtam dtua ayng
to injure (vt)	ทำให้บาดเจ็บ	tham hâi bàat jèp
injury	การบาดเจ็บ	gaan bàat jèp
wound	แผล	phlǎe
trauma	แผลบาดเจ็บ	phlǎe bàat jèp

to be delirious	คลุ้มคลั่ง	khlúm khlâng
to stutter (vi)	พูดตะกุกตะกัก	phôot dtà-gùk-dtà-gàk
sunstroke	โรคลมแดด	rôhk lom dàet

65. Symptoms. Treatments. Part 2

| pain, ache | ความเจ็บปวด | khwaam jèp bpùat |
| splinter (in foot, etc.) | เสี้ยน | sîan |

sweat (perspiration)	เหงื่อ	ngèua
to sweat (perspire)	เหงื่อออก	ngèua òrk
vomiting	การอาเจียน	gaan aa-jian
convulsions	การชัก	gaan chák

pregnant (adj)	ตั้งครรภ์	dtâng khan
to be born	เกิด	gèrt
delivery, labor	การคลอด	gaan khlôrt
to deliver (~ a baby)	คลอดบุตร	khlôrt bùt

abortion	การแท้งบุตร	gaan tháeng bùt
breathing, respiration	การหายใจ	gaan hăai-jai
in-breath (inhalation)	การหายใจเข้า	gaan hăai-jai khâo
out-breath (exhalation)	การหายใจออก	gaan hăai-jai òrk
to exhale (breathe out)	หายใจออก	hăai-jai òrk
to inhale (vi)	หายใจเข้า	hăai-jai khâo
disabled person	คนพิการ	khon phí-gaan
cripple	พิการ	phí-gaan
drug addict	ผู้ติดยาเสพติด	phôo dtìt yaa-sàyp-dtìt
deaf (adj)	หูหนวก	hŏo nùak
mute (adj)	เป็นใบ	bpen bâi
deaf mute (adj)	หูหนวกเป็นใบ้	hŏo nùak bpen bâi
mad, insane (adj)	บ้า	bâa
madman (demented person)	คนบ้า	khon bâa
madwoman	คนบ้า	khon bâa
to go insane	เสียสติ	sĭa sà-dtì
gene	ยีน	yeun
immunity	ภูมิคุมกัน	phoom khúm gan
hereditary (adj)	เป็นกรรมพันธุ์	bpen gam-má-phan
congenital (adj)	แตกำเนิด	dtàe gam-nèrt
virus	เชื้อไวรัส	chéua wai-rát
microbe	จุลินทรีย	jù-lin-see
bacterium	แบคทีเรีย	bàek-tee-ria
infection	การติดเชื้อ	gaan dtìt chéua

66. Symptoms. Treatments. Part 3

hospital	โรงพยาบาล	rohng phá-yaa-baan
patient	ผู้ป่วย	phôo bpùay
diagnosis	การวินิจฉัยโรค	gaan wí-nít-chăi rôhk
cure	การรักษา	gaan rák-săa
medical treatment	การรักษา ทางการแพทย์	gaan rák-săa thaang gaan phâet
to get treatment	รับการรักษา	ráp gaan rák-săa
to treat (~ a patient)	รักษา	rák-săa
to nurse (look after)	รักษา	rák-săa
care (nursing ~)	การดูแลรักษา	gaan doo lae rák-săa
operation, surgery	การผ่าตัด	gaan phàa dtàt
to bandage (head, limb)	พันแผล	phan phlăe
bandaging	การพันแผล	gaan phan phlăe
vaccination	การฉีดวัคซีน	gaan chèet wák-seen
to vaccinate (vt)	ฉีดวัคซีน	chèet wák-seen

injection, shot	การฉีดยา	gaan chèet yaa
to give an injection	ฉีดยา	chèet yaa

attack	มีอาการเฉียบพลัน	mee aa-gaan chìap phlan
amputation	การตัดอวัยวะออก	gaan dtàt a-wai-wá òrk
to amputate (vt)	ตัด	dtàt
coma	อาการโคม่า	aa-gaan khoh-mâa
to be in a coma	อยู่ในอาการโคม่า	yòo nai aa-gaan khoh-mâa
intensive care	หน่วยอภิบาล	nùay à-phí-baan

to recover (~ from flu)	ฟื้นตัว	féun dtua
condition (patient's ~)	อาการ	aa-gaan
consciousness	สติสัมปชัญญะ	sà-dtì săm-bpà-chan-yá
memory (faculty)	ความทรงจำ	khwaam song jam

to pull out (tooth)	ถอน	thŏrn
filling	การอุด	gaan ùt
to fill (a tooth)	อุด	ùt

hypnosis	การสะกดจิต	gaan sà-gòt jìt
to hypnotize (vt)	สะกดจิต	sà-gòt jìt

67. Medicine. Drugs. Accessories

medicine, drug	ยา	yaa
remedy	ยา	yaa
to prescribe (vt)	จ่ายยา	jàai yaa
prescription	ใบสั่งยา	bai sàng yaa

tablet, pill	ยาเม็ด	yaa mét
ointment	ยาทา	yaa thaa
ampule	หลอดยา	lòrt yaa
mixture, solution	ยาส่วนผสม	yaa sùan phà-sŏm
syrup	น้ำเชื่อม	nám chêuam
capsule	ยาเม็ด	yaa mét
powder	ยาผง	yaa phŏng

gauze bandage	ผ้าพันแผล	phâa phan phlăe
cotton wool	สำลี	săm-lee
iodine	ไอโอดีน	ai oh-deen

Band-Aid	พลาสเตอร์	phláat-dtêr
eyedropper	ที่หยอดตา	thêe yòrt dtaa
thermometer	ปรอท	bpa -ròrt
syringe	เข็มฉีดยา	khĕm chèet-yaa

wheelchair	รถเข็นคนพิการ	rót khĕn khon phí-gaan
crutches	ไม้ค้ำยัน	máai khám yan
painkiller	ยาแก้ปวด	yaa gâe bpùat
laxative	ยาระบาย	yaa rá-baai

spirits (ethanol)	เอธานอล	ay-thaa-norn
medicinal herbs	สมุนไพร	sà-mǔn phrai
	ทางการแพทย์	thaang gaan phâet
herbal (~ tea)	สมุนไพร	sà-mǔn phrai

APARTMENT

68. Apartment

apartment	อูพาร์ตเมนต์	a-phâat-mayn
room	ห้อง	hôrng
bedroom	ห้องนอน	hôrng norn
dining room	ห้องรับประทานอาหาร	hôrng ráp bprà-thaan aa-hǎan
living room	ห้องนั่งเล่น	hôrng nâng lên
study (home office)	ห้องทำงาน	hôrng tham ngaan
entry room	ห้องเข้า	hôrng khâo
bathroom (room with a bath or shower)	ห้องน้ำ	hôrng náam
half bath	ห้องส้วม	hôrng sûam
ceiling	เพดาน	phay-daan
floor	พื้น	phéun
corner	มุม	mum

69. Furniture. Interior

furniture	เครื่องเรือน	khrêuang reuan
table	โต๊ะ	dtó
chair	เก้าอี้	gâo-êe
bed	เตียง	dtiang
couch, sofa	โซฟา	soh-faa
armchair	เก้าอี้เท้าแขน	gâo-êe tháo khǎen
bookcase	ตู้หนังสือ	dtôo nǎng-sěu
shelf	ชั้นวาง	chán waang
wardrobe	ตู้เสื้อผ้า	dtôo sêua phâa
coat rack (wall-mounted ~)	ที่แขวนเสื้อ	thêe khwǎen sêua
coat stand	ไม้แขวนเสื้อ	mái khwǎen sêua
bureau, dresser	ตู้ลิ้นชัก	dtôo lín chák
coffee table	โต๊ะกาแฟ	dtó gaa-fae
mirror	กระจก	grà-jòk
carpet	พรม	phrom
rug, small carpet	พรมเช็ดเท้า	phrom chét tháo
fireplace	เตาผิง	dtao phǐng

| candle | เทียน | thian |
| candlestick | เชิงเทียน | cherng thian |

drapes	ผ้าแขวน	phâa khwǎen
wallpaper	วอลเปเปอร์	worn-bpay-bper
blinds (jalousie)	บานเกล็ดหน้าต่าง	baan glèt nâa dtàang

table lamp	โคมไฟตั้งโต๊ะ	khohm fai dtâng dtó
wall lamp (sconce)	ไฟติดผนัง	fai dtìt phà-nǎng
floor lamp	โคมไฟตั้งพื้น	khohm fai dtâng phéun
chandelier	โคมระย้า	khohm rá-yáa

leg (of chair, table)	ขา	khǎa
armrest	ที่พักแขน	thêe phák khǎen
back (backrest)	พนักพิง	phá-nák phing
drawer	ลิ้นชัก	lín chák

70. Bedding

bedclothes	ชุดผ้าปูที่นอน	chút phâa bpoo thêe norn
pillow	หมอน	mǒrn
pillowcase	ปลอกหมอน	bplòk mǒrn
duvet, comforter	ผ้าห่วย	phâa phǔay
sheet	ผ้าปู	phâa bpoo
bedspread	ผ้าคลุมเตียง	phâa khlum dtiang

71. Kitchen

kitchen	ห้องครัว	hôrng khrua
gas	แก๊ส	gáet
gas stove (range)	เตาแก๊ส	dtao gàet
electric stove	เตาไฟฟ้า	dtao fai-fáa
oven	เตาอบ	dtao òp
microwave oven	เตาอบไมโครเวฟ	dtao òp mai-khroh-we p

refrigerator	ตู้เย็น	dtôo yen
freezer	ตู้แช่แข็ง	dtôo châe khǎeng
dishwasher	เครื่องลางจาน	khrêuang láang jaan

meat grinder	เครื่องบดเนื้อ	khrêuang bòt néua
juicer	เครื่องคั้น	khrêuang khán
	น้ำผลไม้	náam phǒn-lá-mái
toaster	เครื่องปิ้ง	khrêuang bpîng
	ขนมปัง	khà-nǒm bpang
mixer	เครื่องปั่น	khrêuang bpàn

| coffee machine | เครื่องชงกาแฟ | khrêuang chong gaa-fae |
| coffee pot | หม้อกาแฟ | môr gaa-fae |

coffee grinder	เครื่องบดกาแฟ	khrêuang bòt gaa-fae
kettle	กาน้ำ	gaa náam
teapot	กาน้ำชา	gaa náam chaa
lid	ฝา	fǎa
tea strainer	ที่กรองชา	thêe grorng chaa

spoon	ช้อน	chórn
teaspoon	ช้อนชา	chórn chaa
soup spoon	ช้อนซุป	chórn súp
fork	ส้อม	sôrm
knife	มีด	mêet

tableware (dishes)	ถ้วยชาม	thûay chaam
plate (dinner ~)	จาน	jaan
saucer	จานรอง	jaan rorng

shot glass	แก้วช็อต	gâew chórt
glass (tumbler)	แก้ว	gâew
cup	ถ้วย	thûay

sugar bowl	โถน้ำตาล	thǒh náam dtaan
salt shaker	กระปุกเกลือ	grà-bpùk gleua
pepper shaker	กระปุกพริกไท	grà-bpùk phrík thai
butter dish	ที่ใส่เนย	thêe sài noie

stock pot (soup pot)	หม้อต้ม	môr dtôm
frying pan (skillet)	กระทะ	grà-thá
ladle	กระบวย	grà-buay
colander	กระชอน	grà chorn
tray (serving ~)	ถาด	thàat

bottle	ขวด	khùat
jar (glass)	ขวดโหล	khùat lǒh
can	กระป๋อง	grà-bpǒrng

bottle opener	ที่เปิดขวด	thêe bpèrt khùat
can opener	ที่เปิดกระป๋อง	thêe bpèrt grà-bpǒrng
corkscrew	ที่เปิดจุก	thêe bpèrt jùk
filter	ที่กรอง	thêe grorng
to filter (vt)	กรอง	grorng

| trash, garbage (food waste, etc.) | ขยะ | khà-yà |
| trash can (kitchen ~) | ถังขยะ | thǎng khà-yà |

72. Bathroom

bathroom	ห้องน้ำ	hôrng náam
water	น้ำ	nám
faucet	ก็อกน้ำ	gòk náam

hot water	น้ำร้อน	nám rórn
cold water	น้ำเย็น	nám yen
toothpaste	ยาสีฟัน	yaa sĕe fan
to brush one's teeth	แปรงฟัน	bpraeng fan
toothbrush	แปรงสีฟัน	bpraeng sĕe fan
to shave (vi)	โกน	gohn
shaving foam	โฟมโกนหนวด	fohm gohn nùat
razor	มีดโกน	mêet gohn
to wash (one's hands, etc.)	ล้าง	láang
to take a bath	อาบ	àap
shower	ฝักบัว	fàk bua
to take a shower	อาบน้ำฝักบัว	àap náam fàk bua
bathtub	อ่างอาบน้ำ	àang àap náam
toilet (toilet bowl)	โถชักโครก	thŏh chák khrôhk
sink (washbasin)	อางลางหนา	àang láang-nâa
soap	สบู่	sà-bòo
soap dish	ที่ใส่สบู่	thêe sài sà-bòo
sponge	ฟองน้ำ	forng náam
shampoo	แชมพู	chaem-phoo
towel	ผ้าเช็ดตัว	phâa chét dtua
bathrobe	เสื้อคลุมอาบน้ำ	sêua khlum àap náam
laundry (laundering)	การซักผ้า	gaan sák phâa
washing machine	เครื่องซักผ้า	khrêuang sák phâa
to do the laundry	ซักผ้า	sák phâa
laundry detergent	ผงซักฟอก	phŏng sák-fôrk

73. Household appliances

TV set	ทีวี	thee-wee
tape recorder	เครื่องบันทึกเทป	khrêuang ban-théuk thâyp
VCR (video recorder)	เครื่องบันทึก วิดีโอ	khrêuang ban-théuk wí-dee-oh
radio	วิทยุ	wít-thá-yú
player (CD, MP3, etc.)	เครื่องเล่น	khrêuang lên
video projector	โปรเจ็คเตอร์	bproh-jèk-dtêr
home movie theater	เครื่องฉาย ภาพยนตร์ที่บ้าน	khhrêuang chăai phâap-phá yon thêe bâan
DVD player	เครื่องเล่น DVD	khrêuang lên dee-wee-dee
amplifier	เครื่องขยายเสียง	khrêuang khà-yăi sĭang
video game console	เครื่องเกม คอนโซล	khrêuang gaym khorn sohn
video camera	กล้องถ่ายวิดีโอ	glôrng thàai wí-dee-oh

camera (photo)	กล้องถ่ายรูป	glôrng thàai rôop
digital camera	กลองดิจิตอล	glôrng dì-jì-dton
vacuum cleaner	เครื่องดูดฝุ่น	khrêuang dòot fùn
iron (e.g., steam ~)	เตารีด	dtao rêet
ironing board	กระดานรองรีด	grà-daan rorng rêet
telephone	โทรศัพท์	thoh-rá-sàp
cell phone	มือถือ	meu thěu
typewriter	เครื่องพิมพ์ดีด	khrêuang phim dèet
sewing machine	จักรเย็บผา	jàk yép phâa
microphone	ไมโครโฟน	mai-khroh-fohn
headphones	หูฟัง	hǒo fang
remote control (TV)	รีโมตทีวี	ree môht thee wee
CD, compact disc	CD	see-dee
cassette, tape	เทป	thâyp
vinyl record	จานเสียง	jaan sǐang

THE EARTH. WEATHER

74. Outer space

space	อวกาศ	a-wá-gàat
space (as adj)	ทางอวกาศ	thang a-wá-gàat
outer space	อวกาศ	a-wá-gàat
world	โลก	lôhk
universe	จักรวาล	jàk-grà-waan
galaxy	ดาราจักร	daa-raa jàk
star	ดาว	daao
constellation	กลุ่มดาว	glùm daao
planet	ดาวเคราะห์	daao khrór
satellite	ดาวเทียม	daao thiam
meteorite	ดาวตก	daao dtòk
comet	ดาวหาง	daao hăang
asteroid	ดาวเคราะห์น้อย	daao khrór nói
orbit	วงโคจร	wong khoh-jon
to revolve	เวียน	wian
(~ around the Earth)		
atmosphere	บรรยากาศ	ban-yaa-gàat
the Sun	ดวงอาทิตย์	duang aa-thít
solar system	ระบบสุริยะ	rá-bòp sù-rí-yá
solar eclipse	สุริยุปราคา	sù-rí-yú-bpà-raa-kaa
the Earth	โลก	lôhk
the Moon	ดวงจันทร์	duang jan
Mars	ดาวอังคาร	daao ang-khaan
Venus	ดาวศุกร์	daao sùk
Jupiter	ดาวพฤหัส	daao phá-réu-hàt
Saturn	ดาวเสาร์	daao săo
Mercury	ดาวพุธ	daao phút
Uranus	ดาวยูเรนัส	daao-yoo-ray-nát
Neptune	ดาวเนปจูน	daao-nâyp-joon
Pluto	ดาวพลูโต	daao phloo-dtoh
Milky Way	ทางช้างเผือก	thaang cháang phèuak
Great Bear (Ursa Major)	กลุ่มดาวหมีใหญ่	glùm daao měe yài
North Star	ดาวเหนือ	daao něua

Martian	ชาวดาวอังคาร	chaao daao ang-khaan
extraterrestrial (n)	มนุษย์ต่างดาว	má-nút dtàang daao
alien	มนุษย์ต่างดาว	má-nút dtàang daao
flying saucer	จานบิน	jaan bin

spaceship	ยานอวกาศ	yaan a-wá-gàat
space station	สถานีอวกาศ	sà-thǎa-nee a-wá-gàat
blast-off	การปล่อยจรวด	gaan bplòi jà-rùat

engine	เครื่องยนต์	khrêuang yon
nozzle	ทอไอพ่น	thôr ai phôn
fuel	เชื้อเพลิง	chéua phlerng

cockpit, flight deck	ที่นั่งคนขับ	thêe nâng khon khàp
antenna	เสาอากาศ	sǎo aa-gàat
porthole	ช่อง	chôrng
solar panel	อุปกรณ์พลังงานแสงอาทิตย์	ù-bpà-gon phá-lang ngaan sǎeng aa-thít
spacesuit	ชุดอวกาศ	chút a-wá-gàat

| weightlessness | สภาพไร้น้ำหนัก | sà-phâap rái nám nàk |
| oxygen | อ็อกซิเจน | ók sí jayn |

| docking (in space) | การเทียบท่า | gaan thîap thâa |
| to dock (vi, vt) | เทียบทา | thîap thâa |

observatory	หอดูดาว	hǒr doo daao
telescope	กล้องโทรทรรศน์	glôrng thoh-rá-thát
to observe (vt)	เฝ้าสังเกต	fâo sǎng-gàyt
to explore (vt)	สำรวจ	sǎm-rùat

75. The Earth

the Earth	โลก	lôhk
the globe (the Earth)	ลูกโลก	lôok lôhk
planet	ดาวเคราะห์	daao khrór

atmosphere	บรรยากาศ	ban-yaa-gàat
geography	ภูมิศาสตร์	phoo-mí-sàat
nature	ธรรมชาติ	tham-má-châat

globe (table ~)	ลูกโลก	lôok lôhk
map	แผนที่	phǎen thêe
atlas	หนังสือแผนที่โลก	nǎng-sěu phǎen thêe lôhk

Europe	ยุโรป	yú-ròhp
Asia	เอเชีย	ay-chia
Africa	แอฟริกา	àef-rí-gaa
Australia	ออสเตรเลีย	òrt-dtray-lia
America	อเมริกา	a-may-rí-gaa

North America	อเมริกาเหนือ	a-may-rí-gaa něua
South America	อเมริกาใต้	a-may-rí-gaa dtâi
Antarctica	แอนตาร์กติกา	aen-dtàak-dtì-gaa
the Arctic	อารกติค	àak-dtìk

76. Cardinal directions

north	เหนือ	něua
to the north	ทิศเหนือ	thít něua
in the north	ที่ภาคเหนือ	thêe phâak něua
northern (adj)	ทางเหนือ	thaang něua
south	ใต้	dtâi
to the south	ทิศใต้	thít dtâi
in the south	ที่ภาคใต้	thêe phâak dtâi
southern (adj)	ทางใต้	thaang dtâi
west	ตะวันตก	dtà-wan dtòk
to the west	ทิศตะวันตก	thít dtà-wan dtòk
in the west	ที่ภาคตะวันตก	thêe phâak dtà-wan dtòk
western (adj)	ทางตะวันตก	thaang dtà-wan dtòk
east	ตะวันออก	dtà-wan òrk
to the east	ทิศตะวันออก	thít dtà-wan òrk
in the east	ที่ภาคตะวันออก	thêe phâak dtà-wan òrk
eastern (adj)	ทางตะวันออก	thaang dtà-wan òrk

77. Sea. Ocean

sea	ทะเล	thá-lay
ocean	มหาสมุทร	má-hǎa sà-mùt
gulf (bay)	อ่าว	àao
straits	ช่องแคบ	chôrng khâep
land (solid ground)	พื้นดิน	phéun din
continent (mainland)	ทวีป	thá-wêep
island	เกาะ	gòr
peninsula	คาบสมุทร	khâap sà-mùt
archipelago	หมู่เกาะ	mòo gòr
bay, cove	อ่าว	àao
harbor	ท่าเรือ	thâa reua
lagoon	ลากูน	laa-goon
cape	แหลม	lǎem
atoll	อะทอลล์	à-thorn
reef	แนวปะการัง	naew bpà-gaa-rang

| coral | ปะการัง | bpà gaa-rang |
| coral reef | แนวปะการัง | naew bpà-gaa-rang |

deep (adj)	ลึก	léuk
depth (deep water)	ความลึก	khwaam léuk
abyss	หุบเหวลึก	hùp wǎy léuk
trench (e.g., Mariana ~)	ร่องลึกก้นสมุทร	rông léuk gôn sà-mùt

| current (Ocean ~) | กระแสน้ำ | grà-sǎe náam |
| to surround (bathe) | ล้อมรอบ | lórm rôrp |

| shore | ชายฝั่ง | chaai fàng |
| coast | ชายฝั่ง | chaai fàng |

flow (flood tide)	น้ำขึ้น	náam khêun
ebb (ebb tide)	น้ำลง	náam long
shoal	หาดตื้น	hàat dtêun
bottom (~ of the sea)	ก้นทะเล	gôn thá-lay

wave	คลื่น	khlêun
crest (~ of a wave)	ม้วนคลื่น	múan khlêun
spume (sea foam)	ฟองคลื่น	forng khlêun

storm (sea storm)	พายุ	phaa-yú
hurricane	พายุเฮอร์ริเคน	phaa-yú her-rí-khayn
tsunami	คลื่นยักษ์	khlêun yák
calm (dead ~)	ภาวะไร้ลมพัด	phaa-wá rái lom phát
quiet, calm (adj)	สงบ	sà-ngòp

| pole | ขั้วโลก | khûa lôhk |
| polar (adj) | ขั้วโลก | khûa lôhk |

latitude	เส้นรุ้ง	sên rúng
longitude	เส้นแวง	sên waeng
parallel	เส้นขนาน	sên khà-nǎan
equator	เส้นศูนย์สูตร	sên sǒon sòot

sky	ท้องฟ้า	thórng fáa
horizon	ขอบฟ้า	khòrp fáa
air	อากาศ	aa-gàat

lighthouse	ประภาคาร	bprà-phaa-khaan
to dive (vi)	ดำ	dam
to sink (ab. boat)	จม	jom
treasures	สมบัติ	sǒm-bàt

78. Seas' and Oceans' names

| Indian Ocean | มหาสมุทรอินเดีย | má-hǎa sà-mùt in-dia |
| Pacific Ocean | มหาสมุทรแปซิฟิก | má-hǎa sà-mùt bpae-sí-fík |

Atlantic Ocean	มหาสมุทร แอตแลนติก	má-hǎa sà-mùt àet-laen-dtìk
Arctic Ocean	มหาสมุทรอาร์คติก	má-hǎa sà-mùt aa-ká-dtìk
Black Sea	ทะเลดำ	thá-lay dam
Red Sea	ทะเลแดง	thá-lay daeng
Yellow Sea	ทะเลเหลือง	thá-lay lěuang
White Sea	ทะเลขาว	thá-lay khǎao
Caspian Sea	ทะเลแคสเปียน	thá-lay khâet-bpian
Dead Sea	ทะเลเดดซี	thá-lay dàyt-see
Mediterranean Sea	ทะเลเมดิเตอรเรเนียน	thá-lay may-dì-dtêr-ray-nian
Aegean Sea	ทะเลเอเจี้ยน	thá-lay ay-jîan
Adriatic Sea	ทะเลเอเดรียติก	thá-lay ay-day-ree-yá-dtìk
Arabian Sea	ทะเลอาหรับ	thá-lay aa-ràp
Sea of Japan	ทะเลญี่ปุ่น	thá-lay yêe-bpùn
Bering Sea	ทะเลเบริ่ง	thá-lay bae-rîng
South China Sea	ทะเลจีนใต้	thá-lay jeen-dtâi
Coral Sea	ทะเลคอรัล	thá-lay khor-ran
Tasman Sea	ทะเลแทสมัน	thá-lay thâet man
Caribbean Sea	ทะเลแคริบเบียน	thá-lay khae-ríp-bian
Barents Sea	ทะเลบาเรนท์	thá-lay baa-rayn
Kara Sea	ทะเลคารา	thá-lay khaa-raa
North Sea	ทะเลเหนือ	thá-lay něua
Baltic Sea	ทะเลบอลติก	thá-lay bon-dtìk
Norwegian Sea	ทะเลนอรเวย์	thá-lay nor-rá-way

79. Mountains

mountain	ภูเขา	phoo khǎo
mountain range	ทิวเขา	thiw khǎo
mountain ridge	สันเขา	sǎn khǎo
summit, top	ยอดเขา	yôrt khǎo
peak	ยอด	yôrt
foot (~ of the mountain)	ตีนเขา	dteun khǎo
slope (mountainside)	ไหลเขา	lài khǎo
volcano	ภูเขาไฟ	phoo khǎo fai
active volcano	ภูเขาไฟมีพลัง	phoo khǎo fai mee phá-lang
dormant volcano	ภูเขาไฟที่ดับแล้ว	phoo khǎo fai thêe dàp láew
eruption	ภูเขาไฟระเบิด	phoo khǎo fai rá-bèrt

crater	ปล่องภูเขาไฟ	bplòng phoo khǎo fai
magma	หินหนืด	hǐn nèut
lava	ลาวา	laa-waa
molten (~ lava)	หลอมเหลว	lǒrm lěo

canyon	หุบเขาลึก	hùp khǎo léuk
gorge	ซองเขา	chôrng khǎo
crevice	รอยแตกภูเขา	roi dtàek phoo khǎo
abyss (chasm)	หุบเหวลึก	hùp wǎy léuk

pass, col	ทางผ่าน	thaang phàan
plateau	ที่ราบสูง	thêe râap sǒong
cliff	หน้าผา	nâa phǎa
hill	เนินเขา	nern khǎo

glacier	ธารน้ำแข็ง	thaan náam khǎeng
waterfall	น้ำตก	nám dtòk
geyser	น้ำพุร้อน	nám phú rórn
lake	ทะเลสาบ	thá-lay sàap

plain	ที่ราบ	thêe râap
landscape	ภูมิทัศน์	phoom thát
echo	เสียงสะท้อน	sǐang sà-thón

alpinist	นักปีนเขา	nák bpeen khǎo
rock climber	นักไต่เขา	nák dtài khǎo
to conquer (in climbing)	ไต่เขาถึงยอด	dtài khǎo thěung yôt
climb (an easy ~)	การปีนเขา	gaan bpeen khǎo

80. Mountains names

The Alps	เทือกเขาแอลป์	thêuak-khǎo-aen
Mont Blanc	ยอดเขามงบล็อง	yôt khǎo mong-bà-lǒng
The Pyrenees	เทือกเขาไพรีนีส	thêuak khǎo pai-ree-nêet

The Carpathians	เทือกเขา คาร์เพเทียน	thêuak khǎo khaa-phay-thian
The Ural Mountains	เทือกเขายูรัล	thêuak khǎo yoo-ran
The Caucasus Mountains	เทือกเขาคอเคซัส	thêuak khǎo khor-khay-sát
Mount Elbrus	ยอดเขาเอลบรุส	yôt khǎo ayn-brùt

The Altai Mountains	เทือกเขาอัลไต	thêuak khǎo an-dtai
The Tian Shan	เทือกเขาเทียนชาน	thêuak khǎo thian-chaan
The Pamir Mountains	เทือกเขาพาเมียร์	thêuak khǎo paa-mia

| The Himalayas | เทือกเขาหิมาลัย | thêuak khǎo hì-maa-lai |
| Mount Everest | ยอดเขาเอเวอเรสต์ | yôt khǎo ay-wer-râyt |

| The Andes | เทือกเขาแอนดีส | thêuak-khǎo-aen-dèet |
| Mount Kilimanjaro | ยอดเขาคิลิมันจาโร | yôt khǎo khí-lí-man-jaa-roh |

81. Rivers

river	แม่น้ำ	mâe náam
spring (natural source)	แหล่งน้ำแร่	làeng náam râe
riverbed (river channel)	เส้นทางแม่น้ำ	sên thaang mâe náam
basin (river valley)	ลุ่มน้ำ	lûm náam
to flow into ...	ไหลไปสู่...	lăi bpai sòo...
tributary	สาขา	săa-khăa
bank (of river)	ฝั่งแม่น้ำ	fàng mâe náam
current (stream)	กระแสน้ำ	grà-săe náam
downstream (adv)	ตามกระแสน้ำ	dtaam grà-săe náam
upstream (adv)	ทวนน้ำ	thuan náam
inundation	น้ำท่วม	nám thûam
flooding	น้ำท่วม	nám thûam
to overflow (vi)	เอ่อล้น	èr lón
to flood (vt)	ท่วม	thûam
shallow (shoal)	บริเวณน้ำตื้น	bor-rí-wayn nám dtêun
rapids	กระแสน้ำเชี่ยว	grà-săe nám-chîeow
dam	เขื่อน	khèuan
canal	คลอง	khlorng
reservoir (artificial lake)	ที่เก็บกักน้ำ	thêe gèp gàk náam
sluice, lock	ประตูระบายน้ำ	bprà-dtoo rá-baai náam
water body (pond, etc.)	พื้นน้ำ	phéun náam
swamp (marshland)	บึง	beung
bog, marsh	ห้วย	hûay
whirlpool	น้ำวน	nám won
stream (brook)	ลำธาร	lam thaan
drinking (ab. water)	น้ำดื่มได้	nám dèum dâai
fresh (~ water)	น้ำจืด	nám jèut
ice	น้ำแข็ง	nám khăeng
to freeze over (ab. river, etc.)	แช่แข็ง	châe khăeng

82. Rivers' names

Seine	แม่น้ำเซน	mâe náam sayn
Loire	แม่น้ำลัวร์	mâe-náam lua
Thames	แม่น้ำเทมส์	mâe-náam them
Rhine	แม่น้ำไรน์	mâe-náam rai
Danube	แม่น้ำดานูบ	mâe-náam daa-nôop

Volga	แม่น้ำวอลกา	mâe-náam won-gaa
Don	แม่น้ำดอน	mâe-náam don
Lena	แม่น้ำลีนา	mâe-náam lee-naa

Yellow River	แม่น้ำหวง	mâe-náam hǔang
Yangtze	แม่น้ำแยงซี	mâe-náam yaeng-see
Mekong	แม่น้ำโขง	mâe-náam khǒhng
Ganges	แม่น้ำคงคา	mâe-náam khong-khaa

Nile River	แม่น้ำไนล์	mâe-náam nai
Congo River	แม่น้ำคองโก	mâe-náam khong-goh
Okavango River	แม่น้ำ โอคาวังโก	mâe-náam oh-khaa wang goh
Zambezi River	แม่น้ำแซมบีซี	mâe-náam saem bee see
Limpopo River	แม่น้ำลิมโปโป	mâe-náam lim-bpoh-bpoh
Mississippi River	แม่น้ำ มิสซิสซิปปี	mâe-náam mít-sít-síp-bpee

83. Forest

| forest, wood | ป่าไม้ | bpàa máai |
| forest (as adj) | ป่า | bpàa |

thick forest	ป่าทึบ	bpàa théup
grove	ป่าละเมาะ	bpàa lá-mór
forest clearing	ทุ่งโล่ง	thûng lôhng

| thicket | ป่าละเมาะ | bpàa lá-mór |
| scrubland | ป่าละเมาะ | bpàa lá-mór |

| footpath (troddenpath) | ทางเดิน | thaang dern |
| gully | ร่องธาร | rôhng thaan |

tree	ต้นไม้	dtôn máai
leaf	ใบไม้	bai máai
leaves (foliage)	ใบไม้	bai máai

fall of leaves	ใบไม้ร่วง	bai máai rûang
to fall (ab. leaves)	ร่วง	rûang
top (of the tree)	ยอด	yôrt

branch	กิ่ง	gìng
bough	กานไม้	gâan mái
bud (on shrub, tree)	ยอดออน	yôrt òrn
needle (of pine tree)	เข็ม	khěm
pine cone	ลูกสน	lôok sǒn

tree hollow	โพรงไม้	phrohng máai
nest	รัง	rang
burrow (animal hole)	โพรง	phrohng

trunk	ลำต้น	lam dtôn
root	ราก	râak
bark	เปลือกไม้	bplèuak máai
moss	มอส	môt

to uproot (remove trees or tree stumps)	ถอนราก	thŏrn râak
to chop down	โค่น	khôhn
to deforest (vt)	ตัดไม้ทำลายป่า	dtàt mái tham laai bpàa
tree stump	ตอไม้	dtor máai

campfire	กองไฟ	gorng fai
forest fire	ไฟป่า	fai bpàa
to extinguish (vt)	ดับไฟ	dàp fai

forest ranger	เจ้าหน้าที่ดูแลป่า	jâo nâa-thêe doo lae bpàa
protection	การปกป้อง	gaan bpòk bpôrng
to protect (~ nature)	ปกป้อง	bpòk bpôrng
poacher	นักลอบล่าสัตว์	nák lôrp lâa sàt
steel trap	กับดักเหล็ก	gàp dàk lèk

| to gather, to pick (vt) | เก็บ | gèp |
| to lose one's way | หลงทาง | lŏng thaang |

84. Natural resources

natural resources	ทรัพยากรธรรมชาติ	sáp-pá-yaa-gon tham-má-châat
minerals	แร่	râe
deposits	ตะกอน	dtà-gorn
field (e.g., oilfield)	บ่อ	bòr

to mine (extract)	ขุดแร่	khùt râe
mining (extraction)	การขุดแร่	gaan khùt râe
ore	แร่	râe
mine (e.g., for coal)	เหมืองแร่	mĕuang râe
shaft (mine ~)	ช่องเหมือง	chôrng mĕuang
miner	คนงานเหมือง	khon ngaan mĕuang

| gas (natural ~) | แก๊ส | gáet |
| gas pipeline | ท่อแก๊ส | thôr gáet |

oil (petroleum)	น้ำมัน	nám man
oil pipeline	ท่อน้ำมัน	thôr náam man
oil well	บ่อน้ำมัน	bòr náam man
derrick (tower)	ปั้นจั่นขนาดใหญ่	bpân jàn khà-nàat yài
tanker	เรือบรรทุกน้ำมัน	reua ban-thúk nám man

| sand | ทราย | saai |
| limestone | หินปูน | hĭn bpoon |

gravel	กรวด	grùat
peat	พีต	phêet
clay	ดินเหนียว	din nǐeow
coal	ถ่านหิน	thàan hǐn
iron (ore)	เหล็ก	lèk
gold	ทอง	thorng
silver	เงิน	ngern
nickel	นิเกิล	ní-gêrn
copper	ทองแดง	thorng daeng
zinc	สังกะสี	sǎng-gà-sěe
manganese	แมงกานีส	maeng-gaa-nêet
mercury	ปรอท	bpa -ròrt
lead	ตะกั่ว	dtà-gùa
mineral	แร่	râe
crystal	ผลึก	phà-lèuk
marble	หินอ่อน	hǐn òrn
uranium	ยูเรเนียม	yoo-ray-niam

85. Weather

weather	สภาพอากาศ	sà-phâap aa-gàat
weather forecast	พยากรณ์ สภาพอากาศ	phá-yaa-gon sà-phâap aa-gàat
temperature	อุณหภูมิ	un-hà-phoom
thermometer	ปรอทวัดอุณหภูมิ	bpà-ròrt wát un-hà-phoom
barometer	เครื่องวัดความดัน บรรยากาศ	khrêuang wát khwaam dan ban-yaa-gàat
humid (adj)	ชื้น	chéun
humidity	ความชื้น	khwaam chéun
heat (extreme ~)	ความร้อน	khwaam rórn
hot (torrid)	ร้อน	rórn
it's hot	มันร้อน	man rórn
it's warm	มันอุ่น	man ùn
warm (moderately hot)	อุ่น	ùn
it's cold	อากาศเย็น	aa-gàat yen
cold (adj)	เย็น	yen
sun	ดวงอาทิตย์	duang aa-thít
to shine (vi)	ส่องแสง	sòrng sǎeng
sunny (day)	มีแสงแดด	mee sǎeng dàet
to come up (vi)	ขึ้น	khêun
to set (vi)	ตก	dtòk
cloud	เมฆ	mâyk

cloudy (adj)	มีเมฆมาก	mee mâyk mâak
rain cloud	เมฆฝน	mâyk fŏn
somber (gloomy)	มืดครึ้ม	mêut khréum

rain	ฝน	fŏn
it's raining	ฝนตก	fŏn dtòk
rainy (~ day, weather)	ฝนตก	fŏn dtòk
to drizzle (vi)	ฝนปรอย	fòn bproi

pouring rain	ฝนตกหนัก	fŏn dtòk nàk
downpour	ฝนหาใหญ่	fŏn hàa yài
heavy (e.g., ~ rain)	หนัก	nàk
puddle	หลมน้ำ	lòm nám
to get wet (in rain)	เปียก	bpìak

fog (mist)	หมอก	mòrk
foggy	หมอกจัด	mòrk jàt
snow	หิมะ	hì-má
it's snowing	หิมะตก	hì-má dtòk

86. Severe weather. Natural disasters

thunderstorm	พายุฟ้าคะนอง	phaa-yú fáa khá-nong
lightning (~ strike)	ฟ้าผา	fáa phàa
to flash (vi)	แลบ	lâep

thunder	ฟ้าคะนอง	fáa khá-norng
to thunder (vi)	มีฟ้าคะนอง	mee fáa khá-norng
it's thundering	มีฟ้าร้อง	mee fáa rórng

| hail | ลูกเห็บ | lôok hèp |
| it's hailing | มีลูกเห็บตก | mee lôok hèp dtòk |

| to flood (vt) | ท่วม | thûam |
| flood, inundation | น้ำทวม | nám thûam |

earthquake	แผ่นดินไหว	phàen din wǎi
tremor, shoke	ไหว	wǎi
epicenter	จุดเหนือศูนย์แผ่นดินไหว	jùt něua sǒon phàen din wǎi

| eruption | ภูเขาไฟระเบิด | phoo khǎo fai rá-bèrt |
| lava | ลาวา | laa-waa |

twister	พายุหมุน	phaa-yú mǔn
tornado	พายุทอร์เนโด	phaa-yú thor-nay-doh
typhoon	พายุไต้ฝุ่น	phaa-yú dtâi fùn

| hurricane | พายุเฮอร์ริเคน | phaa-yú her-rí-khayn |
| storm | พายุ | phaa-yú |

tsunami	คลื่นสึนามิ	khlêun sèu-naa-mí
cyclone	พายุไซโคลน	phaa-yú sai-khlohn
bad weather	อากาศไม่ดี	aa-gàat mâi dee
fire (accident)	ไฟไหม้	fai mâi
disaster	ความหายนะ	khwaam hǎa-yá-ná
meteorite	อุกกาบาต	ùk-gaa-bàat

avalanche	หิมะถล่ม	hì-má thà-lòm
snowslide	หิมะถลม	hì-má thà-lòm
blizzard	พายุหิมะ	phaa-yú hì-má
snowstorm	พายุหิมะ	phaa-yú hì-má

FAUNA

87. Mammals. Predators

predator	สัตว์กินเนื้อ	sàt gin néua
tiger	เสือ	sěua
lion	สิงโต	sǐng dtoh
wolf	หมาป่า	mǎa bpàa
fox	หมาจิ้งจอก	mǎa jîng-jòk
jaguar	เสือจากัวร์	sěua jaa-gua
leopard	เสือดาว	sěua daao
cheetah	เสือชีตาห์	sěua chee-dtaa
black panther	เสือดำ	sěua dam
puma	สิงโตภูเขา	sǐng-dtoh phoo khǎo
snow leopard	เสือดาวหิมะ	sěua daao hì-má
lynx	แมวป่า	maew bpàa
coyote	โคโยตี้	khoh-yoh-dtêe
jackal	หมาจิ้งจอกทอง	mǎa jîng-jòk thorng
hyena	ไฮยีนา	hai-yee-naa

88. Wild animals

animal	สัตว์	sàt
beast (animal)	สัตว์	sàt
squirrel	กระรอก	grà rôk
hedgehog	เมน	mâyn
hare	กระต่ายป่า	grà-dtàai bpàa
rabbit	กระต่าย	grà-dtàai
badger	แบดเจอร์	baet-jer
raccoon	แร็คคูน	ráek khoon
hamster	หนูแฮมสเตอร์	nǒo haem-sà-dtêr
marmot	มาร์มอต	maa-môt
mole	ตุ่น	dtùn
mouse	หนู	nǒo
rat	หนู	nǒo
bat	ค้างคาว	kháang khaao
ermine	เออร์มิน	er-min
sable	เซเบิล	say bern

marten	มาร์เทิน	maa thern
weasel	เพียงพอน	phiang phon
	สีน้ำตาล	sěe nǎm dtaan
mink	เพียงพอน	phiang phorn
beaver	บีเวอร์	bee-wer
otter	นาก	nâak
horse	ม้า	máa
moose	กวางมูส	gwaang môot
deer	กวาง	gwaang
camel	อูฐ	òot
bison	วัวป่า	wua bpàa
wisent	วัวป่าออรอช	wua bpàa or rôt
buffalo	ควาย	khwaai
zebra	มาลาย	máa laai
antelope	แอนที่โลป	aen-thi-lòp
roe deer	กวางโรเดียร์	gwaang roh-dia
fallow deer	กวางแฟลโลว์	gwaang flae-loh
chamois	เลียงผา	liang-phǎa
wild boar	หมูป่า	mǒo bpàa
whale	วาฬ	waan
seal	แมวน้ำ	maew náam
walrus	ช้างน้ำ	cháang náam
fur seal	แมวน้ำมีขน	maew náam mee khǒn
dolphin	โลมา	loh-maa
bear	หมี	měe
polar bear	หมีขั้วโลก	měe khúa lôhk
panda	หมีแพนดา	měe phaen-dâa
monkey	ลิง	ling
chimpanzee	ลิงชิมแปนซี	ling chim-bpaen-see
orangutan	ลิงอุรังอุตัง	ling u-rang-u-dtang
gorilla	ลิงกอริลลา	ling gor-rin-lâa
macaque	ลิงแม็กแคก	ling mâk-khâk
gibbon	ชะนี	chá-nee
elephant	ช้าง	cháang
rhinoceros	แรด	râet
giraffe	ยีราฟ	yee-râaf
hippopotamus	ฮิปโปโปเตมัส	híp-bpoh-bpoh-dtay-mát
kangaroo	จิงโจ้	jing-jôh
koala (bear)	หมีโคอาล่า	měe khoh aa lâa
mongoose	พังพอน	phang phon
chinchilla	ดินคิลลา	khin-khin laa
skunk	สกุ๊งก	sà-gang
porcupine	เม่น	mâyn

89. Domestic animals

cat	แมวตัวเมีย	maew dtua mia
tomcat	แมวตัวผู้	maew dtua phôo
dog	สุนัข	sù-nák
horse	ม้า	máa
stallion (male horse)	ม้าตัวผู้	máa dtua phôo
mare	มาตัวเมีย	máa dtua mia
cow	วัว	wua
bull	กระทิง	grà-thing
ox	วัว	wua
sheep (ewe)	แกะตัวเมีย	gàe dtua mia
ram	แกะตัวผู้	gàe dtua phôo
goat	แพะตัวเมีย	pháe dtua mia
billy goat, he-goat	แพะตัวผู้	pháe dtua phôo
donkey	ลา	laa
mule	ลอ	lôr
pig, hog	หมู	mǒo
piglet	ลูกหมู	lôok mǒo
rabbit	กระต่าย	grà-dtàai
hen (chicken)	ไก่ตัวเมีย	gài dtua mia
rooster	ไก่ตัวผู้	gài dtua phôo
duck	เป็ดตัวเมีย	bpèt dtua mia
drake	เป็ดตัวผู้	bpèt dtua phôo
goose	ห่าน	hàan
tom turkey, gobbler	ไก่งวงตัวผู้	gài nguang dtua phôo
turkey (hen)	ไก่งวงตัวเมีย	gài nguang dtua mia
domestic animals	สัตว์เลี้ยง	sàt líang
tame (e.g., ~ hamster)	เลี้ยง	líang
to tame (vt)	เชื่อง	chêuang
to breed (vt)	ขยายพันธุ์	khà-yǎai phan
farm	ฟาร์ม	faam
poultry	สัตว์ปีก	sàt bpèek
cattle	วัวควาย	wua khwaai
herd (cattle)	ฝูง	fǒong
stable	คอกม้า	khôrk máa
pigpen	คอกหมู	khôrk mǒo
cowshed	คอกวัว	khôrk wua
rabbit hutch	คอกกระต่าย	khôrk grà-dtàai
hen house	เล้าไก่	láo gài

90. Birds

bird	นก	nók
pigeon	นกพิราบ	nók phí-râap
sparrow	นกกระจิบ	nók grà-jìp
tit (great tit)	นกติ๊ด	nók dtít
magpie	นกสาลิกา	nók sǎa-lí gaa

raven	นกอีกา	nók ee-gaa
crow	นกกา	nók gaa
jackdaw	นกจำพวกกา	nók jam phúak gaa
rook	นกการูค	nók gaa róok

duck	เป็ด	bpèt
goose	ห่าน	hàan
pheasant	ไก่ฟ้า	gài fáa

eagle	นกอินทรี	nók in-see
hawk	นกเหยี่ยว	nók yìeow
falcon	นกเหยี่ยว	nók yìeow
vulture	นกแร้ง	nók ráeng
condor (Andean ~)	นกแร้งขนาดใหญ่	nók ráeng kà-nàat yài

swan	นกหงส์	nók hǒng
crane	นกกระเรียน	nók grà rian
stork	นกกระสา	nók grà-sǎa

parrot	นกแก้ว	nók gâew
hummingbird	นกฮัมมิ่งเบิร์ด	nók ham-mîng-bèrt
peacock	นกยูง	nók yoong

ostrich	นกกระจอกเทศ	nók grà-jòrk-thâyt
heron	นกยาง	nók yaang
flamingo	นกฟลามิงโก	nók flaa-ming-goh
pelican	นกกระทุง	nók-grà-thung

| nightingale | นกไนติงเกล | nók-nai-dting-gayn |
| swallow | นกนางแอ่น | nók naang-àen |

thrush	นกเดินดง	nók dern dong
song thrush	นกเดินดงรองเพลง	nók dern dong rórng phlayng
blackbird	นกเดินดงสีดำ	nók-dern-dong sěe dam

swift	นกแอ่น	nók àen
lark	นกลาร์ค	nók lâak
quail	นกคุ่ม	nók khúm

woodpecker	นกหัวขวาน	nók hǔa khwǎan
cuckoo	นกดุเหว่า	nók dù hǎy wâa
owl	นกฮูก	nók hôok

eagle owl	นกฮูกเค้าใหญ่	nók kháo yài
wood grouse	ไก่ป่า	gài bpàa
black grouse	ไก่ดำ	gài dam
partridge	นกกระทา	nók-grà-thaa

starling	นกกิ้งโครง	nók-gîng-khrohng
canary	นกขมิ้น	nók khà-mîn
hazel grouse	ไก่น้ำตาล	gài nám dtaan
chaffinch	นกจาบ	nók-jàap
bullfinch	นกบูลฟินช์	nók boon-fin

seagull	นกนางนวล	nók naang-nuan
albatross	นกอัลบาทรอส	nók an-baa-thrôt
penguin	นกเพนกวิน	nók phayn-gwin

91. Fish. Marine animals

bream	ปลาบรีม	bplaa bpreem
carp	ปลาคาร์ป	bplaa khâap
perch	ปลาเพิร์ช	bplaa phêrt
catfish	ปลาดุก	bplaa-dùk
pike	ปลาไพค์	bplaa phai

| salmon | ปลาแซลมอน | bplaa saen-morn |
| sturgeon | ปลาสเตอร์เจี้ยน | bpláa sà-dtêr jian |

herring	ปลาเฮอร์ริง	bplaa her-ring
Atlantic salmon	ปลาแซลมอนแอตแลนติก	bplaa saen-mon àet-laen-dtìk
mackerel	ปลาซาบะ	bplaa saa-bà
flatfish	ปลาลิ้นหมา	bplaa lín-mǎa

zander, pike perch	ปลาไพค์เพิร์ช	bplaa phái phert
cod	ปลาค็อด	bplaa khót
tuna	ปลาทูน่า	bplaa thoo-nâa
trout	ปลาเทราท์	bplaa thrau

eel	ปลาไหล	bplaa lǎi
electric ray	ปลากระเบนไฟฟ้า	bplaa grà-bayn-fai-fáa
moray eel	ปลาไหลมอเรย์	bplaa lǎi mor-ray
piranha	ปลาปิรันยา	bplaa bpì-ran-yâa

shark	ปลาฉลาม	bplaa chà-lǎam
dolphin	โลมา	loh-maa
whale	วาฬ	waan

crab	ปู	bpoo
jellyfish	แมงกะพรุน	maeng gà-phrun
octopus	ปลาหมึก	bplaa mèuk
starfish	ปลาดาว	bplaa daao

| sea urchin | หอยเม่น | hŏi mâyn |
| seahorse | ม้าน้ำ | máa nám |

oyster	หอยนางรม	hŏi naang rom
shrimp	กุ้ง	gúng
lobster	กุ้งมังกร	gúng mang-gon
spiny lobster	กุ้งมังกร	gúng mang-gon

92. Amphibians. Reptiles

| snake | งู | ngoo |
| venomous (snake) | พิษ | phít |

viper	งูแมวเซา	ngoo maew sao
cobra	งูเห่า	ngoo hào
python	งูเหลือม	ngoo lĕuam
boa	งูโบอา	ngoo boh-aa

grass snake	งูเล็กที่ไม่เป็นอันตราย	ngoo lék thêe mâi bpen an-dtà-raai
rattle snake	งูหางกระดิ่ง	ngoo hăang grà-dìng
anaconda	งูอนาคอนดา	ngoo a -naa-khon-daa

lizard	กิ้งก่า	gîng-gàa
iguana	อีกัวนา	ee gua naa
monitor lizard	กิ้งก่ามอนิเตอร์	gîng-gàa mor-ní-dtêr
salamander	ซาลาแมนเดอร์	saa-laa-maen-dêr
chameleon	กิ้งก่าคามิเลียน	gîng-gàa khaa-mí-lian
scorpion	แมงป่อง	maeng bpòrng

turtle	เต่า	dtào
frog	กบ	gòp
toad	คางคก	khaang-kók
crocodile	จระเข้	jor-rá-khây

93. Insects

insect, bug	แมลง	má-laeng
butterfly	ผีเสื้อ	phĕe sêua
ant	มด	mót
fly	แมลงวัน	má-laeng wan
mosquito	ยุง	yung
beetle	แมลงปีกแข็ง	má-laeng bpèek khăeng

wasp	ต่อ	dtòr
bee	ผึ้ง	phêung
bumblebee	ผึ้งบัมเบิลบี	phêung bam-bern bee
gadfly (botfly)	เหลือบ	lèuap

spider	แมงมุม	maeng mum
spiderweb	ใยแมงมุม	yai maeng mum

dragonfly	แมลงปอ	má-laeng bpor
grasshopper	ตั๊กแตน	dták-gà-dtaen
moth (night butterfly)	ผีเสื้อกลางคืน	phěe sêua glaang kheun

cockroach	แมลงสาบ	má-laeng sàap
tick	เห็บ	hèp
flea	หมัด	màt
midge	ริ้น	rín

locust	ตั๊กแตน	dták-gà-dtaen
snail	หอยทาก	hǒi thâak
cricket	จิ้งหรีด	jîng-rèet
lightning bug	หิ่งห้อย,	hìng-hôi
ladybug	แมลงเต่าทอง	má-laeng dtào thorng
cockchafer	แมงอีนูน	maeng ee noon

leech	ปูลิง	bpling
caterpillar	บุ้ง	búng
earthworm	ไส้เดือน	sâi deuan
larva	ตัวอ่อน	dtua òrn

FLORA

94. Trees

tree	ต้นไม้	dtôn máai
deciduous (adj)	ผลัดใบ	phlàt bai
coniferous (adj)	สน	sŏn
evergreen (adj)	ซึ่งเขียวชอุ่ม	sêung khĭeow chá-ùm
	ตลอดปี	dtà-lòrt bpee
apple tree	ต้นแอปเปิ้ล	dtôn àep-bpêrn
pear tree	ต้นแพร	dtôn phae
sweet cherry tree	ต้นเชอร์รี่ป่า	dtôn cher-rêe bpàa
sour cherry tree	ต้นเชอร์รี่	dtôn cher-rêe
plum tree	ตนพลัม	dtôn phlam
birch	ต้นเบิร์ช	dtôn bèrt
oak	ต้นโอ๊ค	dtôn óhk
linden tree	ต้นไมดอกเหลือง	dtôn máai dòrk lĕuang
aspen	ต้นแอสเพน	dtôn ae sà-phayn
maple	ตนเมเปิล	dtôn may bpêrn
spruce	ต้นเฟอร์	dtôn fer
pine	ต้นเกี๊ยะ	dtôn gía
larch	ต้นลารช	dtôn lâat
fir tree	ต้นเฟอร์	dtôn fer
cedar	ตนซีดาร์	dtôn-see-daa
poplar	ต้นปอปลาร์	dtôn bpor-bplaa
rowan	ต้นโรแวน	dtôn-roh-waen
willow	ต้นวิลโลว	dtôn win-loh
alder	ตนอัลเดอร์	dtôn an-dêr
beech	ต้นบีช	dtôn bèet
elm	ต้นเอลม	dtôn elm
ash (tree)	ต้นแอช	dtôn aesh
chestnut	ตนเกาลัด	dtôn gao lát
magnolia	ต้นแมกโนเลีย	dtôn mâek-noh-lia
palm tree	ต้นปาลม	dtôn bpaam
cypress	ตนไซเปรส	dtôn-sai-bpràyt
mangrove	ต้นโกงกาง	dtôn gohng gaang
baobab	ต้นเบาบับ	dtôn bao-bàp
eucalyptus	ต้นยูคาลิปตัส	dtôn yoo-khaa-líp-dtàt
sequoia	ตนสนซีด้วยา	dtôn sŏn see kua yaa

95. Shrubs

bush	พุ่มไม้	phúm máai
shrub	ต้นไม้พุ่ม	dtôn máai phúm
grapevine	ต้นองุ่น	dtôn a-ngùn
vineyard	ไร่องุ่น	râi a-ngùn
raspberry bush	พุ่มราสเบอร์รี่	phúm râat-ber-rêe
blackcurrant bush	พุ่มแบล็คเคอร์แรนท์	phúm blàek-khêr-raen
redcurrant bush	พุ่มเรดเคอร์แรนท์	phúm râyt-khêr-raen
gooseberry bush	พุ่มกูสเบอร์รี่	phúm gòot-ber-rêe
acacia	ต้นอาเคเชีย	dtôn aa-khay-chia
barberry	ต้นบาร์เบอร์รี่	dtôn baa-ber-rêe
jasmine	มะลิ	má-lí
juniper	ต้นจูนิเปอร์	dtôn joo-ní-bper
rosebush	พุ่มกุหลาบ	phúm gù làap
dog rose	พุ่มด็อกโรส	phúm dòrk-rôht

96. Fruits. Berries

fruit	ผลไม้	phŏn-lá-máai
fruits	ผลไม้	phŏn-lá-máai
apple	แอปเปิ้ล	àep-bpêrn
pear	ลูกแพร	lôok phae
plum	พลัม	phlam
strawberry (garden ~)	สตรอว์เบอร์รี่	sà-dtror-ber-rêe
sour cherry	เชอร์รี่	cher-rêe
sweet cherry	เชอร์รี่ป่า	cher-rêe bpàa
grape	องุ่น	a-ngùn
raspberry	ราสเบอร์รี่	râat-ber-rêe
blackcurrant	แบล็คเคอร์แรนท์	blàek khêr-raen
redcurrant	เรดเคอร์แรนท์	râyt-khêr-raen
gooseberry	กูสเบอร์รี่	gòot-ber-rêe
cranberry	แครนเบอร์รี่	khraen-ber-rêe
orange	ส้ม	sôm
mandarin	ส้มแมนดาริน	sôm maen daa rin
pineapple	สับปะรด	sàp-bpà-rót
banana	กล้วย	glúay
date	อินทผลัม	in-thá-phâ-lam
lemon	เลมอน	lay-mon
apricot	แอปริคอท	ae-bprì-khôrt

peach	ลูกท้อ	lôok thór
kiwi	กีวี	gee wee
grapefruit	สมโอ	sôm oh

berry	เบอร์รี่	ber-rêe
berries	เบอร์รี่	ber-rêe
cowberry	คาวเบอร์รี่	khaao-ber-rêe
wild strawberry	สตรอวเบอร์รี่ป่า	sá-dtrorw ber-rêe bpàa
bilberry	บิลเบอร์รี่	bil-ber-rêe

97. Flowers. Plants

| flower | ดอกไม้ | dòrk máai |
| bouquet (of flowers) | ช่อดอกไม้ | chôr dòrk máai |

rose (flower)	ดอกกุหลาบ	dòrk gù làap
tulip	ดอกทิวลิป	dòrk thiw-líp
carnation	ดอกคาร์เนชั่น	dòrk khaa-nay-chân
gladiolus	ดอกแกลดิโอลัส	dòrk gaen-dì-oh-lát

cornflower	ดอกคอร์นฟลาวเวอร์	dòrk khon-flaao-wer
harebell	ดอกระฆัง	dòrk rá-khang
dandelion	ดอกแดนดิไลออน	dòrk daen-dì-lai-on
camomile	ดอกคาโมมายล์	dòrk khaa-moh maai

aloe	ว่านหางจระเข้	wâan-hǎang-jor-rá-khây
cactus	ตะบองเพชร	dtà-bong-phét
rubber plant, ficus	ต้นเลียบ	dtôn lîap

lily	ดอกลิลลี่	dòrk lí-lêe
geranium	ดอกเจอราเนียม	dòrk jer-raa-niam
hyacinth	ดอกไฮอะซินท์	dòrk hai-a-sin

mimosa	ดอกไมยราบ	dòrk mai râap
narcissus	ดอกนาร์ซิสซัส	dòrk naa-sít-sát
nasturtium	ดอกแนสเตอร์ชัม	dòrk nâet-dtêr-cham

orchid	ดอกกล้วยไม้	dòrk glúay máai
peony	ดอกโบตั๋น	dòrk boh-dtǎn
violet	ดอกไวโอเล็ต	dòrk wai-oh-lét

pansy	ดอกแพนนุชี	dòrk phaen-see
forget-me-not	ดอกฟอรเก็ตมีน็อต	dòrk for-gèt-mee-nót
daisy	ดอกเดซี่	dòrk day see

poppy	ดอกป๊อปปี้	dòrk bpóp-bpêe
hemp	กัญชา	gan chaa
mint	สะระแหน่	sà-rá-nàe
lily of the valley	ดอกลิลลี่แห่ง หุบเขา	dòrk lí-lá-lêe hàeng hùp khǎo

snowdrop	ดอกหยาดหิมะ	dòrk yàat hì-má
nettle	ตำแย	dtam-yae
sorrel	ซอรเรล	sor-rayn
water lily	บัว	bua
fern	เฟิร์น	fern
lichen	ไลเคน	lai-khayn
conservatory (greenhouse)	เรือนกระจก	reuan grà-jòk
lawn	สนามหญ้า	sà-nǎam yâa
flowerbed	สนามดอกไม้	sà-nǎam-dòrk-máai
plant	พืช	phêut
grass	หญ้า	yâa
blade of grass	ใบหญ้า	bai yâa
leaf	ใบไม้	bai máai
petal	กลีบดอก	glèep dòrk
stem	ลำต้น	lam dtôn
tuber	หัวใต้ดิน	hǔa dtâi din
young plant (shoot)	ต้นอ่อน	dtôn òrn
thorn	หนาม	nǎam
to blossom (vi)	บาน	baan
to fade, to wither	เหี่ยว	hìeow
smell (odor)	กลิ่น	glìn
to cut (flowers)	ตัด	dtàt
to pick (a flower)	เด็ด	dèt

98. Cereals, grains

grain	เมล็ด	má-lét
cereal crops	ธัญพืช	than-yá-phêut
ear (of barley, etc.)	รวงข้าว	ruang khâao
wheat	ข้าวสาลี	khâao sǎa-lee
rye	ข้าวไรย์	khâao rai
oats	ข้าวโอต	khâao óht
millet	ข้าวฟ่าง	khâao fâang
barley	ขาวบารเลย์	khâao baa-lây
corn	ข้าวโพด	khâao-phôht
rice	ข้าว	khâao
buckwheat	บัควีท	bàk-wêet
pea plant	ถั่วลันเตา	thùa-lan-dtao
kidney bean	ถั่วรูปไต	thùa rôop dtai
soy	ถั่วเหลือง	thùa lěuang
lentil	ถั่วเลนทิล	thùa layn thin
beans (pulse crops)	ถั่ว	thùa

COUNTRIES OF THE WORLD

99. Countries. Part 1

Afghanistan	ประเทศอัฟกานิสถาน	bprà-thâyt àf-gaa-nít-thǎan
Albania	ประเทศแอลเบเนีย	bprà-thâyt aen-bay-nia
Argentina	ประเทศอาร์เจนตินา	bprà-thâyt aa-jayn-dtì-naa
Armenia	ประเทศอาร์เมเนีย	bprà-thâyt aa-may-nia
Australia	ประเทศออสเตรเลีย	bprà-thâyt òt-dtray-lia
Austria	ประเทศออสเตรีย	bprà-thâyt òt-dtria
Azerbaijan	ประเทศอาเซอรไบจาน	bprà-thâyt aa-sêr-bai-jaan
The Bahamas	ประเทศบาฮามาส	bprà-thâyt baa-haa-mâat
Bangladesh	ประเทศ บังคลาเทศ	bprà-thâyt bang-khláa-thâyt
Belarus	ประเทศเบลารุส	bprà-thâyt blao-rút
Belgium	ประเทศเบลเยี่ยม	bprà-thâyt bayn-yiam
Bolivia	ประเทศโบลิเวีย	bprà-thâyt boh-lí-wia
Bosnia and Herzegovina	ประเทศบอสเนีย และเฮอรเซโกวินา	bprà-thâyt bòt-nia láe her-say-goh-wí-naa
Brazil	ประเทศบราซิล	bprà-thâyt braa-sin
Bulgaria	ประเทศบัลแกเรีย	bprà-thâyt ban-gae-ria
Cambodia	ประเทศกัมพูชา	bprà-thâyt gam-phoo-chaa
Canada	ประเทศแคนาดา	bprà-thâyt khae-naa-daa
Chile	ประเทศชิลี	bprà-thâyt chí-lee
China	ประเทศจีน	bprà-thâyt jeen
Colombia	ประเทศโคลัมเบีย	bprà-thâyt khoh-lam-bia
Croatia	ประเทศโครเอเชีย	bprà-thâyt khroh-ay-chia
Cuba	ประเทศคิวบา	bprà-thâyt khiw-baa
Cyprus	ประเทศไซปรัส	bprà-thâyt sai-bpràt
Czech Republic	ประเทศเช็กเกีย	bprà-thâyt chék-gia
Denmark	ประเทศเดนมาร์ก	bprà-thâyt dayn-màak
Dominican Republic	สาธารณรัฐ โดมินิกัน	sǎa-thaa-rá-ná rát doh-mí-ní-gan
Ecuador	ประเทศเอกวาดอร์	bprà-thâyt ay-gwaa-dor
Egypt	ประเทศ อียิปต	bprà-thâyt bprà-thâyt ee-yíp
England	ประเทศอังกฤษ	bprà-thâyt ang-grìt
Estonia	ประเทศเอสโตเนีย	bprà-thâyt àyt-dtoh-nia
Finland	ประเทศฟินแลนด	bprà-thâyt fin-laen
France	ประเทศฝรั่งเศส	bprà-thâyt fà-ràng-sàyt
French Polynesia	เฟรนชโปลินีเซีย	frayn-bpoh-lí-nee-sia
Georgia	ประเทศจอรเจีย	bprà-thâyt jor-jia
Germany	ประเทศเยอรมนี	bprà-thâyt yer-rá-ma-nee

Ghana	ประเทศกานา	bprà-thâyt gaa-naa
Great Britain	บริเตนใหญ่	brì-dtayn yài
Greece	ประเทศกรีซ	bprà-thâyt grèet
Haiti	ประเทศเฮติ	bprà-thâyt hay-dtì
Hungary	ประเทศฮังการี	bprà-thâyt hang-gaa-ree

100. Countries. Part 2

Iceland	ประเทศไอซ์แลนด์	bprà-thâyt ai-laen
India	ประเทศอินเดีย	bprà-thâyt in-dia
Indonesia	ประเทศอินโดนีเซีย	bprà-thâyt in-doh-nee-sia
Iran	ประเทศอิหราน	bprà-thâyt i-ràan
Iraq	ประเทศอิรัก	bprà-thâyt i-rák
Ireland	ประเทศไอรแลนด์	bprà-thâyt ai-laen
Israel	ประเทศอิสราเอล	bprà-thâyt ìt-sà-rǎa-ayn
Italy	ประเทศอิตาลี	bprà-thâyt i-dtaa-lee

Jamaica	ประเทศจาเมกา	bprà-thâyt jaa-may-gaa
Japan	ประเทศญี่ปุ่น	bprà-thâyt yêe-bpùn
Jordan	ประเทศจอรแดน	bprà-thâyt jor-daen
Kazakhstan	ประเทศ คาซัคสถาน	bprà-thâyt khaa-sák--à-thǎan
Kenya	ประเทศเคนย่า	bprà-thâyt khayn-yâa
Kirghizia	ประเทศ คีรกีซสถาน	bprà-thâyt khee-gèet--à-thǎan
Kuwait	ประเทศดูเวต	bprà-thâyt khoo-wâyt

Laos	ประเทศลาว	bprà-thâyt laao
Latvia	ประเทศลัตเวีย	bprà-thâyt lát-wia
Lebanon	ประเทศเลบานอน	bprà-thâyt lay-baa-non
Libya	ประเทศลิเบีย	bprà-thâyt lí-bia
Liechtenstein	ประเทศ ลิกเตนสไตน์	bprà-thâyt lík-tay-ná-sà-dtai
Lithuania	ประเทศลิทัวเนีย	bprà-thâyt lí-thua-nia
Luxembourg	ประเทศลักเซมเบิร์ก	bprà-thâyt lák-saym-bèrk

Macedonia (Republic of ~)	ประเทศมาซิโดเนีย	bprà-thâyt maa-sí-doh-nia
Madagascar	ประเทศ มาดากัสการ์	bprà-thâyt maa-daa-gàt-gaa
Malaysia	ประเทศมาเลเซีย	bprà-thâyt maa-lay-sia
Malta	ประเทศมอลตา	bprà-thâyt mon-dtaa
Mexico	ประเทศเม็กซิโก	bprà-thâyt mék-sí-goh
Moldova, Moldavia	ประเทศมอลโดวา	bprà-thâyt mon-doh-waa

Monaco	ประเทศโมนาโก	bprà-thâyt moh-naa-goh
Mongolia	ประเทศมองโกเลีย	bprà-thâyt mong-goh-lia
Montenegro	ประเทศ มอนเตเนโกร	bprà-thâyt mon-dtay-nay-groh
Morocco	ประเทศมอร็อคโค	bprà-thâyt mor-rók-khoh
Myanmar	ประเทศเมียนมาร	bprà-thâyt mian-maa

Namibia	ประเทศนามิเบีย	bprà-thâyt naa-mí-bia
Nepal	ประเทศเนปาล	bprà-thâyt nay-bpaan
Netherlands	ประเทศเนเธอร์แลนด์	bprà-thâyt nay-ther-laen
New Zealand	ประเทศนิวซีแลนด์	bprà-thâyt niw-see-laen
North Korea	เกาหลีเหนือ	gao-lĕe nĕua
Norway	ประเทศนอร์เวย์	bprà-thâyt nor-way

101. Countries. Part 3

Pakistan	ประเทศ ปากีสถาน	bprà-thâyt bpaa-gèet-thăan
Palestine	ปาเลสไตน์	bpaa-lâyt-dtai
Panama	ประเทศปานามา	bprà-thâyt bpaa-naa-maa
Paraguay	ประเทศปารากวัย	bprà-thâyt bpaa-raa-gwai
Peru	ประเทศเปรู	bprà-thâyt bpay-roo
Poland	ประเทศโปแลนด์	bprà-thâyt bpoh-laen
Portugal	ประเทศโปรตุเกส	bprà-thâyt bproh-dtù-gàyt
Romania	ประเทศโรมาเนีย	bprà-thâyt roh-maa-nia
Russia	ประเทศรัสเซีย	bprà-thâyt rát-sia
Saudi Arabia	ประเทศ ซาอุดีอาระเบีย	bprà-thâyt saa-u-dì aa-ra--bia
Scotland	ประเทศสก็อตแลนด์	bprà-thâyt sà-gòt-laen
Senegal	ประเทศเซเนกัล	bprà-thâyt say-nay-gan
Serbia	ประเทศเซอร์เบีย	bprà-thâyt sêr-bia
Slovakia	ประเทศสโลวาเกีย	bprà-thâyt sà-loh-waa-gia
Slovenia	ประเทศสโลวีเนีย	bprà-thâyt sà-loh-wee-nia
South Africa	ประเทศแอฟริกาใต้	bprà-thâyt àef-rí-gaa dtâi
South Korea	เกาหลีใต้	gao-lĕe dtâi
Spain	ประเทศสเปน	bprà-thâyt sà-bpayn
Suriname	ประเทศซูรินาม	bprà-thâyt soo-rí-naam
Sweden	ประเทศสวีเดน	bprà-thâyt sà-wĕe-dayn
Switzerland	ประเทศสวิตเซอร์แลนด์	bprà-thâyt sà-wìt-sêr-laen
Syria	ประเทศซีเรีย	bprà-thâyt see-ria
Taiwan	ไต้หวัน	dtâi-wăn
Tajikistan	ประเทศทาจิกิสถาน	bprà-thâyt thaa-jì-gìt-thăan
Tanzania	ประเทศแทนซาเนีย	bprà-thâyt thaen-saa-nia
Tasmania	ประเทศแทสเมเนีย	bprà-thâyt thâet-may-nia
Thailand	ประเทศไทย	bprà-tâyt thai
Tunisia	ประเทศตูนิเซีย	bprà-thâyt dtoo-ní-sia
Turkey	ประเทศตุรกี	bprà-thâyt dtù-rá-gee
Turkmenistan	ประเทศ เติร์กเมนิสถาน	bprà-thâyt dtèrk-may-nít-thăan
Ukraine	ประเทศยูเครน	bprà-thâyt yoo-khrayn
United Arab Emirates	สหรัฐอาหรับเอมิเรตส์	sà-hà-rát aa-ràp ay-mí-râyt
United States of America	สหรัฐอเมริกา	sà-hà-rát a-may-rí-gaa
Uruguay	ประเทศอุรุกวัย	bprà-thâyt u-rúk-wai

Uzbekistan	ประเทศอุซเบกิสถาน	bprà-thâyt ùt-bay-gìt-thǎan
Vatican	นครรัฐวาติกัน	ná-khon rát waa-dtì-gan
Venezuela	ประเทศเวเนซุเอลา	bprà-thâyt way-nay-sú-ay-laa
Vietnam	ประเทศเวียดนาม	bprà-thâyt wîat-naam
Zanzibar	ประเทศแซนซิบาร์	bprà-thâyt saen-sí-baa

THAI
VOCABULARY

FOR ENGLISH SPEAKERS

ENGLISH-
THAI

The most useful words
To expand your lexicon and sharpen
your language skills

3000 words

T&p BOOKS

Thai vocabulary for English speakers - 3000 words
By Andrey Taranov

T&P Books vocabularies are intended for helping you learn, memorize and review foreign words. The dictionary is divided into themes, covering all major spheres of everyday activities, business, science, culture, etc.

The process of learning words using T&P Books' theme-based dictionaries gives you the following advantages:

- Correctly grouped source information predetermines success at subsequent stages of word memorization
- Availability of words derived from the same root allowing memorization of word units (rather than separate words)
- Small units of words facilitate the process of establishing associative links needed for consolidation of vocabulary
- Level of language knowledge can be estimated by the number of learned words

T&P Books Publishing
www.tpbooks.com

ISBN: 978-1-78767-230-7

This book is also available in E-book formats.
Please visit www.tpbooks.com or the major online bookstores.